# To the *Pointe*

## A guide toward fulfilling a dancer's ability to rise successfully en pointe

Copyright © 2014, Carol Reeder. All rights reserved.

Except as permitted under the U.S. Copyright Act of 1976, no part of this publication may be reproduced, distributed, or transmitted in any form or by any means, or stored in a database or retrieval system, without the prior written permission of the publisher; exceptions are made for brief excerpts in published reviews.

ISBN-13: 978-1-937458-85-0

Printed in the United States of America.

This publication is designed to provide entertainment value and is sold with the understanding that the publisher is not engaged in rendering legal, accounting, or other professional advice of any kind. If legal advice or other expert assistance is required, the services of a competent professional person should be sought.

—From a Declaration of Principles jointly adopted by a Committee of the American Bar Association and a Committee of Publishers and Associations

# To the *Pointe*

## A guide toward fulfilling a dancer's ability to rise successfully en pointe

Carol Reeder

Much as the caterpillar becomes a butterfly, through proper care and training, so emerges a dancer to take flight and soar.

# Mission Statement

As well as existing in a continual state of change, each dancer has her own strengths, weaknesses and habits, which need to be recognized and managed.

The goal of this book is to empower young dancers with the knowledge and ability to successfully rise en pointe.

# Table of **CONTENTS**

| | | |
|---|---|---|
| 1 | Alignment and Placement | 19 |
| 2 | Feet and Ankles | 37 |
| 3 | Knees and Legs | 67 |
| 4 | Hips and Turnout | 103 |
| 5 | Core and Back | 121 |
| 6 | Balance, Pirouette and Arabesque | 137 |
| 7 | About Pointe | 157 |
| 8 | Miscellaneous Information and Daily Improvement Sheets | 171 |
| | Acknowledgments | 191 |
| | Bibliography | 192 |
| | Our Dancers | 194 |
| | About the Author | 195 |
| | Preparing For Your Assessments | 197 |

# What Skills Will You Need for POINTE?

The basic requirements to rise confidently and safely en pointe are strong, flexible feet, ankles, and legs with excellent placement, fantastic core control, and a primary understanding of anatomy and how your body works. A list of 36 tests have been established to ensure you can reach these skills. These tests have been developed by others as well as myself, and passing them demonstrates a dancer's readiness to proceed to the next level.

Every dancer's body is unique, having its own challenges and abilities toward fulfilling each requirement within this book. Some tests may be easily passed. Some, you may find very hard depending on your body build, strengths and skills. There are, however, no shortcuts, only diligent daily work on exercises needed for improvement, the determination to complete each requirement and the knowledge that your hard work will be rewarded.

# QUALIFYING Steps

From the six levels listed on the following page, the first four to master are covered within this book. The 5th one must be determined by your pre-pointe teacher and the final one, by your doctor.

- » **Pre-Pointe Class Goals**
  A list of the achievements you answer for yourself. Honestly address each item and check them off as you master them. They work hand in hand with your assessment tests and may uncover weaknesses you were not aware you had.

- » **Pre-Pointe Assessments**
  The actual tests you need to pass with your examiner. When you can do all 36 of these tests, you have successfully completed this course leaving items 5 and 6 to fulfill before you actually are ready to purchase your first pointe shoes.

> Knowing your own body and what you can accomplish with it is invaluable and will stay with you the rest of your life. Treat your body well, listen to it, challenge it, and it will respond more than you could ever imagine.

# 6 Points to **Master** Before Being Placed **EN POINTE**

1 **CORRECT ALIGNMENT**
- Can be maintained on two legs whether in standing, elevé or during pliés.
- Can be maintained on one leg whether in standing, elevé or plié.

2 **FOOT, ANKLE and LEG STRENGTH/FLEXIBILITY**

Demonstrate your ability to:
- Both pointe and elevé to the range required for pointe work.
- Plié deeply, equally, and correctly.
- Elevé to full demi-pointe 20 times.

3 **TORSO AND TURNOUT CONTROL**
- Is maintained on two legs whether elevé or changement.
- Is maintained on one leg in standing whether in standing, elevé or changement.

4 **BALANCING SKILLS**
- Are maintained when standing on one leg or in plié without wobbling or flicking tendons.
- Are maintained in elevé or relevé retiré. Both in parallel and turnout.

6 **DEMONSTRATES THESE SKILLS IN CLASS WORK**
- Continually dances with strength, flexibility, alignment and balance.
- Core, back, shoulder, legs, arms and head are coordinated, controlled and used well.
- Legs and feet are properly stretched and well controlled.
- Turnout is achieved from the hips and continues to improve.

7 **DOCTOR'S APPROVAL— BODY and BONE DEVELOPMENT**
- Growth plates have matured sufficiently for pointe work.
- Scoliosis exam.

# Personal **CHECK LIST**

*How many of these skills have you mastered?*

■ 1   I understand alignment and can center myself whether standing or in elevé on two feet or one foot.

■ 2   My demi-plié is deep, well turned out, equal on both sides, and I hold my knees well over my toes.

■ 3   I can elevé or relevé on both legs to full demi-pointe with straight well pulled up and turned out legs, hold 10 counts without wobbling and return with control.

■ 4   I can elevé or relevé to full demi-pointe on a well pulled up, turned out leg, hold for 3 counts without wobbling and return with control.

■ 5   I use my feet and legs fully and correctly in all tendu and degagé movements.

■ 6   I understand weight placement on my balancing points and correctly apply this understanding in class whether standing on one or two feet, in elevé, or plié.

■ 7   I understand torso alignment and apply it in my dancing whether balancing, turning, or jumping.

■ 8   In grand battement, développé and ronde de jambe en l'air, I manage my legs and hips correcty, maintaining hip and upper body alignment.

■ 9   I understand the difference between elevé, relevé and posé movements.

■ 10   I have the ability to hold my body erect, perform a grand plié center floor and return without wobbling or moving my feet around.

■ 11   I have the ability to hold my toes long when pointing, standing or on demi-pointe without gripping or clawing.

■ 12   Without losing control, I can find center when moving from two feet to one foot during elevé, relevé, posé or sauté movements.

■ 13   I have enough strength to maintain turnout in both legs and attain 90° or higher extension.

■ 14   I have strong feet and ankles that keep me from wobbling while I elevé and lower.

■ 15   Because your attitude drastically determines your progress, do you throughly enjoy ballet and focus on getting the most out of each class?

# Pre-Pointe ASSESSMENTS

**PURPOSE:** To assess through testing, a dancers alignment, strengths, and balancing skills, making sure faulty technique and inadequate strength, flexibility and centering has been corrected and is up to a level necessary for pointe work.

**#1 Standing Posture in 1st**
*aligned, turned out with shoulder blades flat*

**#2 Demi-Plié Alignment in 5th**
*aligned as in #1 with knees over toes in plié*

**#3 Demi-Plié Depth - Right**
*the ability to plié 2 1/2" to 4 1/2"*

**#4 Demi-Plié Depth - Left**
*the ability to plié 2 1/2" to 4 1/2"*

**#5 Elevé Pointe Range - Right**
*line from ankle to big toe's metatarsal is 90° to floor*

**#6 Elevé Pointe Range - Left**
*line from ankle to big toe's metatarsal is 90° to floor*

**#7 Seated Pointe Range - Right**
*line from ankle to big toe's metatarsal is parallel to floor*

**#8 Seated Pointe Range - Left**
*line from ankle to big toe's metatarsal is parallel to floor*

**#9 20 Single Leg Elevés - Right**
*5 counts up - 5 counts down*

**#10 20 Single Leg Elevés - Left**
*5 counts up - 5 counts down*

**#11 Changement - Right front**
*without pulling back, rolling or lifting heels*

**#12 Changement - Left front**
*without pulling back, rolling or lifting heels*

**#13 Single Leg Stand in Plié - Right**
*hold 10 counts without flicking or wobbling*

**#14 Single Leg Stand in Plié - Left**
*hold 10 counts without flicking or wobbling*

**#15 Degagés from 5th - Right**
*4 front. side and back*

**#16 Degagés from 5th - Left**
*4 front. side and back*

**#17 Single Leg Stand in Turnout - Right**
*hold 10 counts without flicking or wobbling*

**#18 Single Leg Stand in Turnout - Left**
*hold 10 counts without flicking or wobbling*

**#19 1 Leg Elevé Retiré Parallel - Right**
*hold 3 counts without wobbling*

**#20 1 Leg Elevé Retiré Parallel - Left**
*hold 3 counts without wobbling*

**#21 1 Leg Elevé Retiré in Turnout - Right**
*hold 3 counts without wobbling*

**#22 1 Leg Elevé Retiré in Turnout - Left**
*hold 3 counts without wobbling*

**#23 Advanced Plank - Right foot on floor**
*hold 10 counts without wobbling*

**#24 Advanced Plank - Left foot on floor**
*hold 10 counts without wobbling*

**#25 Single Leg Sauté in turnout - Right**
*without lifting hip or pulling back*

**#26 Single Leg Sauté in turnout - Left**
*without lifting hip or pulling back*

**#27 Superman with Twist - Right**
*4 counts up, 4 twist R and center, - 5x*

**#28 Superman with Twist - Left**
*4 counts up, 4 twist L and center, - 5x*

**#29 Relevé Retiré in Parallel - Right**
*hold 3 counts without wobbling*

**#30 Relevé Retiré in Parallel - Left**
*hold 3 counts without wobbling*

**#31 Relevé Retiré in Turnout - Right**
*hold 3 counts without wobbling*

**#32 Relevé Retiré in Turnout - Left**
*hold 3 counts without wobbling*

**#33 Posé Développé Devant - R and L**
*hold 3 counts and roll down*

**#34 Posé Retiré à la seconde - R and L**
*hold 3 counts and spring down*

**#35 Arabesque Combination - Right**
*hold 3 counts in arabesque and pirouette ending up without wobbling*

**#36 Arabesque Combination - Left**
*hold 3 counts in arabesque and pirouette ending up without wobbling*

# PHASES IN MOVEMENT

## CONCENTRIC Training
positive contraction

The contracting portion of an exercise is when muscle fibers shorten. As in the upward movement of a grand battement away from gravity.

## ISOMETRIC Training
zero movement

Isometric exercises have no physical movement. The angle of the joint and length of the muscle doesn't change. It's as if trying to move an immovable object.

## ECCENTRIC Training
negative movement

The return with gravity portion of an exercise lengthening the muscle fibers, as in the controlled lowering of a grand battement. An eccentrically-loaded exercise spends more time on the returning phase of a movement.

### Muscle Movement

Each movement phase has its own effect on the muscles, tendons and tissues which surround them.

Concentric = builds strength with less soreness and fatigue.

Isotonic = builds the same muscle strength as concentric exercising without the cardiovascular benefit.

Eccentric = builds greater strength and bulk.

### Sore Muscles

Working a muscle hard causes tiny tears within it. You feel this as sore muscles for a few days. After healing, these sore muscles become stronger.

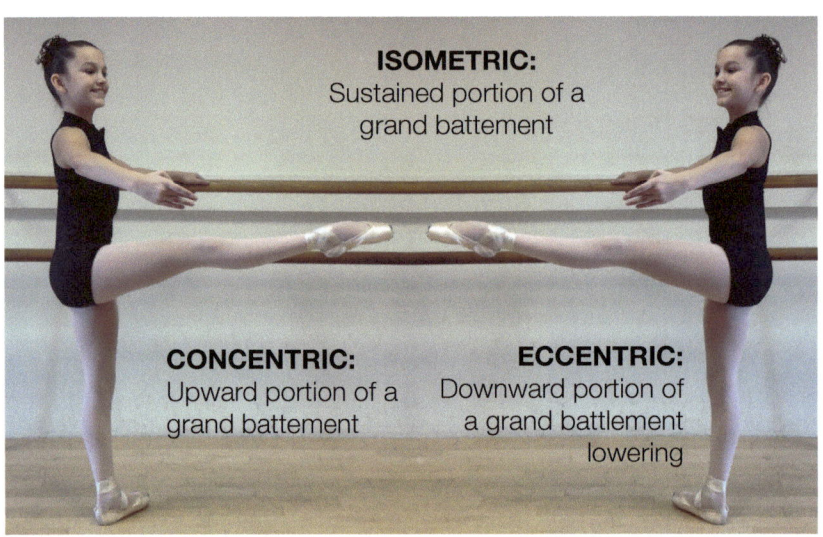

**ISOMETRIC:** Sustained portion of a grand battement

**CONCENTRIC:** Upward portion of a grand battement

**ECCENTRIC:** Downward portion of a grand battlement lowering

Moving a muscle activates only a few of its fibers. Repeating that movement again and again forces a muscle to activate more and more fibers until all fibers of that muscle are being used. In isometric exercise, the muscle quickly activates more and more fibers attempting to move that immovable object. In a matter of seconds, all fibers of that muscle are working with no repetitions.

# MUSCLE TYPES

### Fast Twitch Muscles
like the sprinter - power and speed
Fast twitch fibers are thin, small and produce fast repetitive movements. They are mainly used during the concentric phase of movement and are able to produce both explosive power and speed as in allegro movements.

### Slow Twitch Muscles
like the marathon runner - endurance
Slow twitch fibers give bulk to your muscles and are used during the eccentric phase of movement. They are slow-reacting and made for endurance. These are the muscles which hold our bones in place in and control our posture.

To make things more clear, let's look at the chicken. Like us, they have both types of muscles. Their fast twitch fibers make up the white meat and slow twitch the dark. Their legs, the dark meat, are for walking and standing for long periods of time - slow twitch. The white meat of their chest controls their wings and are for short bursts of activity - fast twitch.

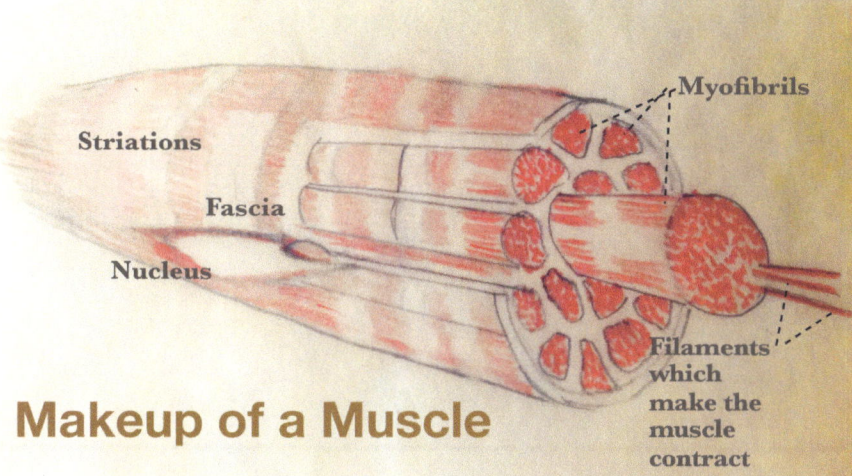

**Makeup of a Muscle**

Two types of muscle fibers, fast twitch and slow twitch, move our body. Each is unique in its ability to contract. Most movement muscles are made of about 50% of each type of fiber.

**FAST TWITCH...**
are muscles which, like a race car, move you fast but burn energy quickly and will fatigue rather quickly.

**SLOW TWITCH...**
are muscles which burn oxygen more efficiently. They fire slower and can hold a contraction for long periods of time before fatiguing.

Each muscle is unique in its fiber makeup and its ability to fire.

# MUSCLE MEMORY

Repeating a pattern over and over creates what we call "Muscle Memory." This is the ability of our body to master a complicated movement pattern and perform it easily, like a pas de chat. When you first learned to do a pas de chat, it was hard. You had to think about where each part of your body needed to be placed during each movement. With practice, your pas de chat became automatic - muscle memory.

Scientifically it's called motor learning, a form of procedural memory. What really happens is that your brain creates a long-term memory pattern. This frees your brain to focus on the combination you're learning rather than each individual step within the combination; as when you store things in your pocket or purse so your hands are free to do something else.

## Incorrectly Repeating a Pattern FORMING BAD HABITS

The hard thing about muscle memory is when you learn something incorrectly, you have to start over retraining those stored memory patterns. Bad habits are mainly formed from repeating patterns with missed information. Somehow you didn't receive or use all the information you needed to perform a step correctly. To avoid forming bad habits in class, pay close attention and practice each movement correctly from the beginning.

## Why is a Step "Correct"?

### HISTORICALLY, MEDICALLY, STYLISTICALLY

Historically: The way a step has come to us from the past, evolving from the labors of its best and most successful dancers and choreographers.

Medically: Anatomical reasons - the way we are built. A simple example is in the use of our knees. Knees are hinge joints which move in one plain to flex or extend our leg. If you force a knee to roll inward or outward constantly, you can stretch and weaken the connecting ligaments. A sudden misplaced landing can tear those ligaments.

Stylistically: What looks best. Style is governed not only by the type of dance you study but by line, balance, direction, flow and any other contributing factor that determines how you look when performing.

# FASCIA AND MUSCLES
## The importance of fascia

Muscles attach to each bone in our body through tendons and control our movements, posture and balance. Fascia, a thin sheet of fibrous connective tissue, not only covers every muscle, tendon and bone, but lies under our skin encasing, binding and weaving its way throughout our entire body. It protects, connects and shapes us. It is mainly made up of tightly-packed collagen fibers which are movable, flexible and resilient. Fascia needs water to stay lubricated.

"Fascia is the missing element in the movement/stability equation," says Tom Myers, medical professional and author of Anatomy Trains. Now, for the latest discovery - fascia actually can contract, feel and respond to stress on its own. Fascia works in your body much like pulling up on the shoulder of your leotard, pulling, stretching and adjusting throughout your entire leotard. Now, pull on your leotard 5,000 times. This is about how many adjustments your fascia would make during a one-hour class.

When fascia is healthy, it is smooth, supple and slides easily, allowing you to stretch in any direction and return back to normal. But injury causes these fibers to thicken in order to protect the underlying muscle. Lack of activity will cement what used to be supple fibers in place with sticky adhesions.

### Keep Stretching MOVE IT OR LOSE IT
If not moved and stretched, our body forms sticky adhesions between fascia and muscles or other surfaces and this limits motion. Once it tightens up, it wants to stay tight. Fascia can withstand up to 2,000 pounds of pressure per square inch, so it doesn't stretch easily. Fascial stretching is done gently for three to five minutes relaxing into the hold. Follow this by rolling the area out with a foam roller or ball, or give the area a good massage and a warm soak.

### Chronic Tightness STAYING TIGHT
When muscles become tight, the fascia surrounding them tightens. As time passes this fascia becomes ridged, compressing the muscles and nerves around it.

### Injury BEWARE
Should you ever become injured and develop a limp or other restricted movement patterns, your fascia will respond. And even after the injury has healed, you could retain that same movement pattern.

# MUSCLE of the Human Body

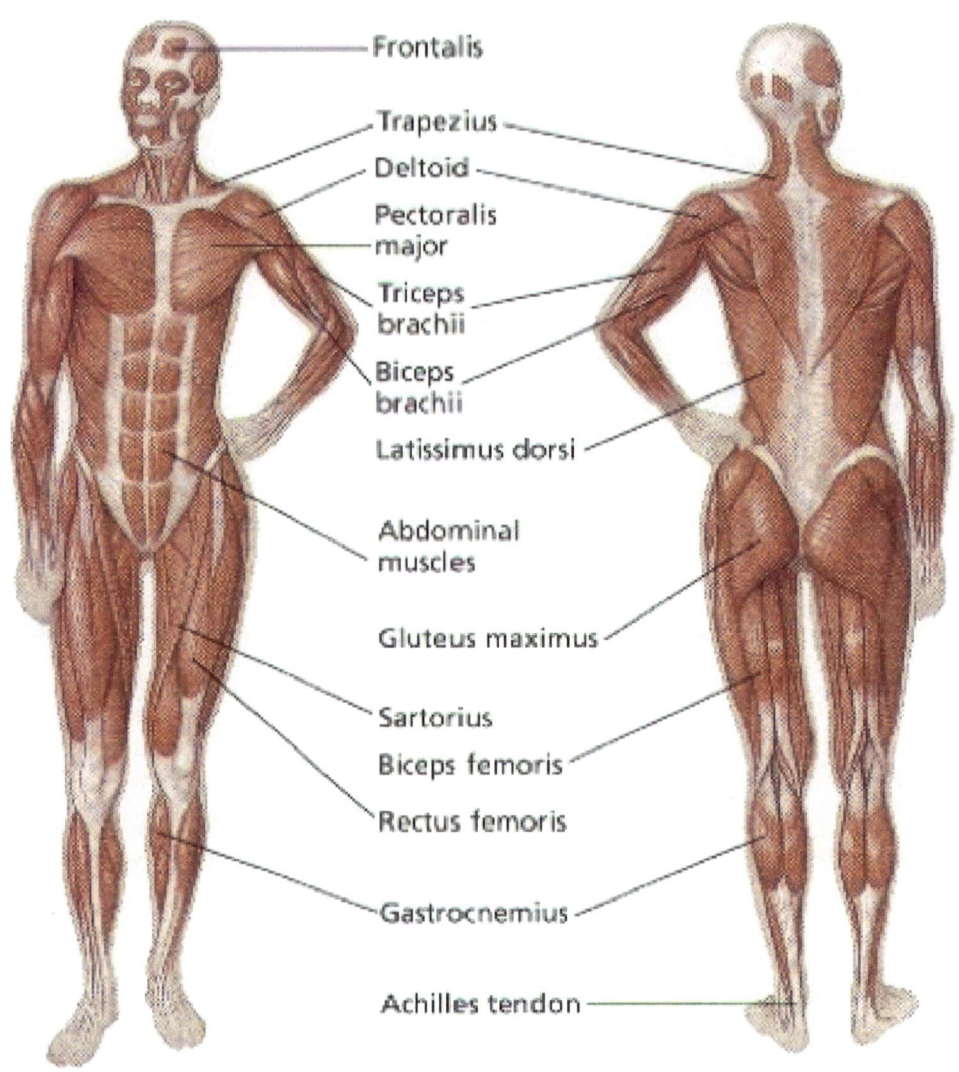

## Basic Terminology

1. **Tendons -** Attach muscle to bone.

2. **Ligaments -** Attach bone to bone (some tightly put together; some stretchy). Strong bands of ligaments surround each of our joints.

3. **Fascia -** A thin, web-like sheeting that covers and permeates our entire body.

4. **Flexibility -** About releasing fascial tension and nerve restriction as well as ligament, tendon, and muscle mobility within and around a joint.

5. **Hyperextention -** About extra joint mobility—going beyond neutral.

6. **Hypoextention -** About less joint mobility—achieving less than neutral.

# THE SKELETAL System

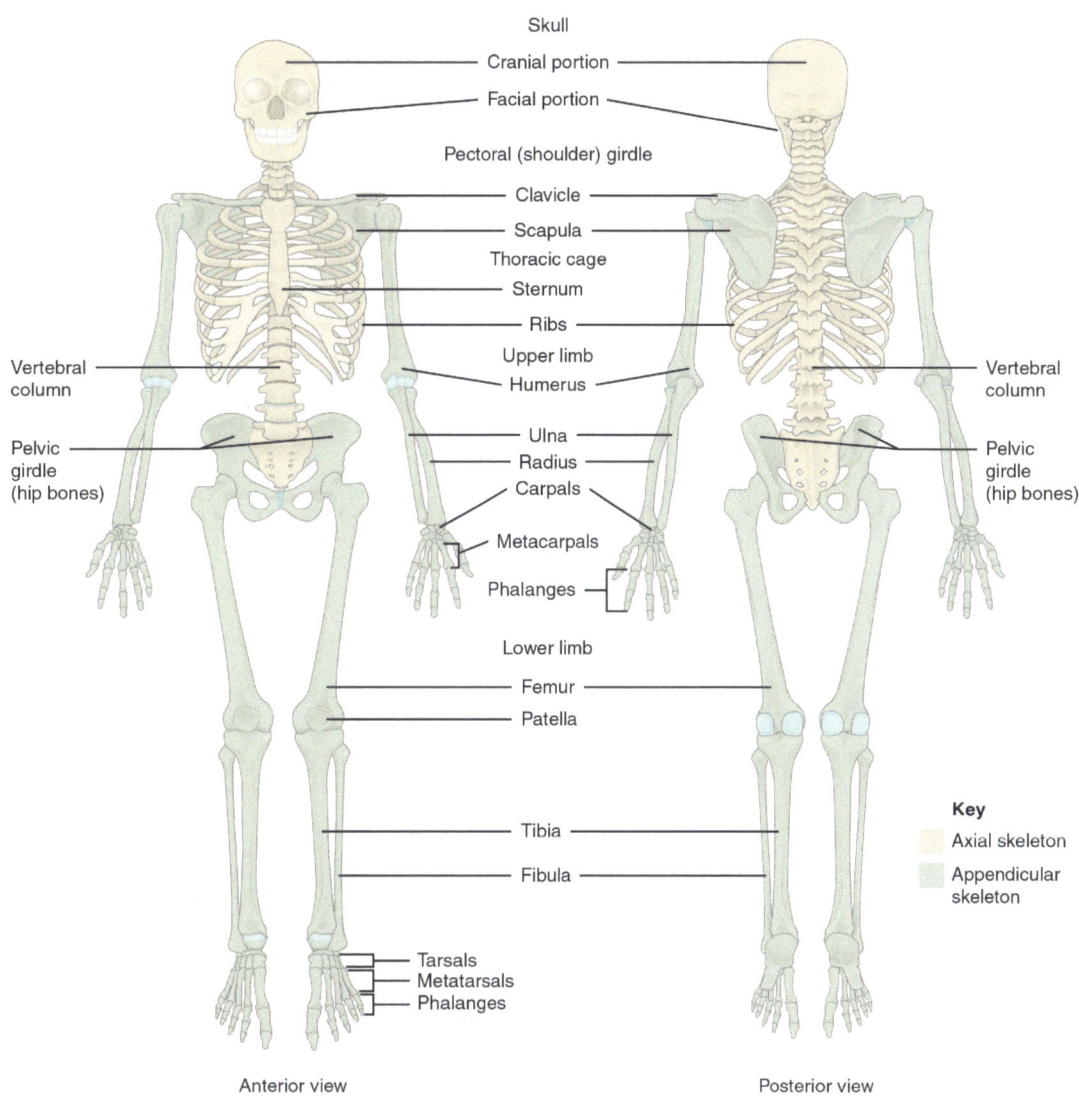

## Types of Joints

1. **Hinge Joint -** Allows movement in one plane, much like a door opening and closing as in your elbows and knees.

2. **Ball and Socket Joint -** Allows twisting/turning movements with a rounded head that turns in its socket. Found in the hip and shoulder.

3. **Gliding Joint -** Allows two flat bones to slide over each other like the ankle and wrist.

4. **Condyloid Joint -** Allows the head to nod and fingers to bend.

5. **Saddle Joint -** Allows the thumb to touch any finger.

# Chapter 1

## ASSESSMENTS 1 - 4

# *Alignment and Placement*

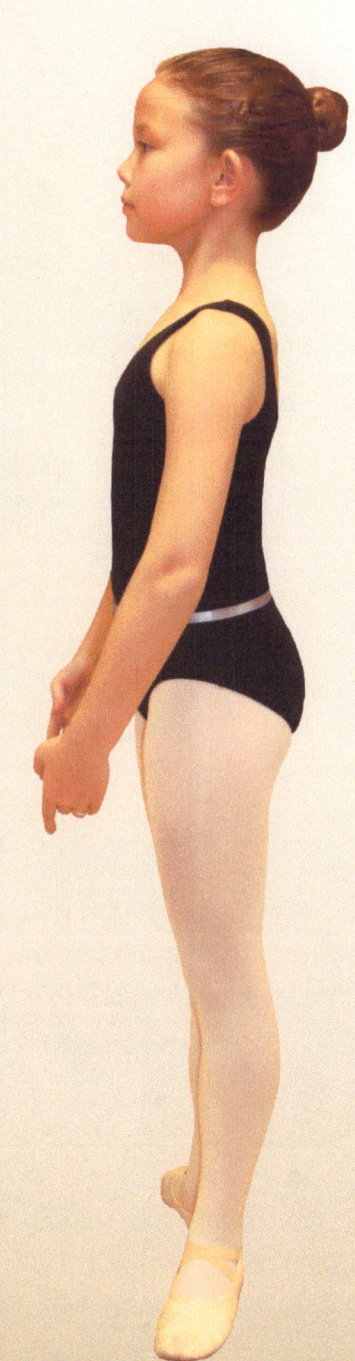

"Posture and dance are interwoven and inseparable. It is reflected in a dancer's carriage, movements, and expression. Poor posture prevents the body from functioning properly because a part or parts are out of alignment, thus causing mechanical shifting which results in excessive muscular effort or even strain."

## NEUTRAL

Considered to be the position of power and balance.

# SUMMARY
## Chapter 1
# ALIGNMENT AND PLACEMENT

Alignment and correct placement are the cornerstones of dance — the foundation from which movement extends, balance is found and turns continue. Stand in front of a full-length mirror and look for any problems you have developed.

### FEET and ANKLES:

Check your feet while standing in each position making sure they don't roll. Now elevé, first on two feet then one. Do you wobble, clench, or claw? Then do lots of exercises to strengthen them. Check your feet when pointing. Make sure they don't sickle (especially in back) and your toes stay long and don't curl under.

### LEGS, HIPS, BACK, RIBS and SHOULDERS:

Check your stance. Can you hold your knees straight, your hips square and your back long, not swayed? Are your ribs held in and down? Are your shoulders down and open? Do you have protruding shoulder blades?

### HEAD, NECK and ARMS:

Check the placement of your head. Do you hold it straight or do you tilt it slightly to one side? Can you hold it straight when you spot? What about your neck and chin, do they poke forward? What about your mouth? Do you pull your lips between your teeth when you are working hard? Now evaluate your arms. Can you hold them strong but not ridged? Do you let your elbows or hands drop? Do you carry your arms too far back or front?

*All these details are important in your development as a dancer.*

### PLACEMENT IN RETIRÉ:

As you lift your foot into retiré, do you raise your hip or even twist it sideways? Does this force your torso to lean to one side? Be sure your hips stay square to the floor and your shoulders remain over them.

### PLACEMENT IN ELEVÉ RETIRÉ:

When you rise to demi-pointe, can you maintain the same squareness and hold your core, back and shoulders in position? Do you rise straight up or do you pull back or to the side? Are you able to hold turnout and stay over your point of balance?

# WEIGHT BEARING Placement

## When Standing On Two Feet (Tripod Stand)

When standing on two feet in any position, your weight is equally divided between the big toe, little toe and heel, forming a tripod balancing platform for each foot.

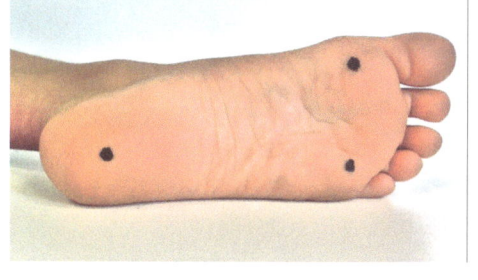

*Correct balancing points when standing on two feet*

## When Standing On One Foot

When standing on one foot, the balancing point moves forward to 60% on the ball of your foot and 40% on the heel. This keeps you from sitting back on your heel and prepares you to elevé. Keeping your weight on your heel places a lot of strain on the front of the shin which pulls on your shin bone.

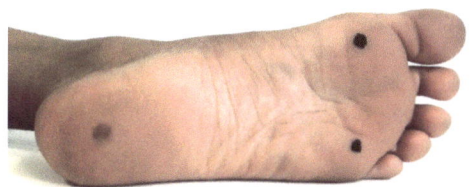

*Correct balancing points on one foot.*

## When Standing In Elevé/Relevé

No matter if you are on one or two feet, your balancing point on each foot in elevé is between your big toe and second toe. This gives you a strong centered base and keeps you from rolling outward (sickling) onto your little toe.

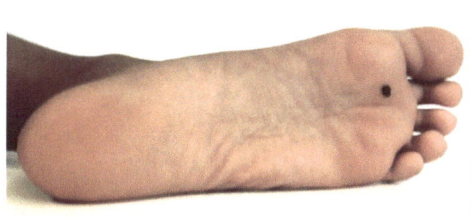

*Correct balancing point in elevé*

## When En Pointe

When you are finally wearing your first pair of pointe shoes and press up, you must rise fully onto the top of the platform and the end pads of your fully stretched toes.

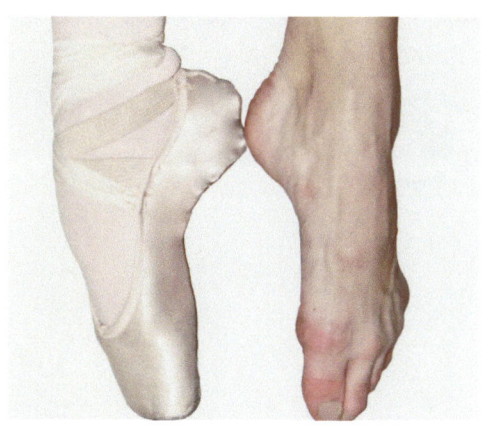

*Correct balancing point in elevé*

# POINTING YOUR Foot

There are three ways of pointing your foot. Only two of these are acceptable in ballet.

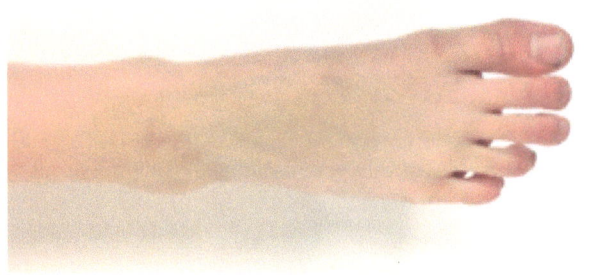

### A Neutral Foot

A foot pointed in neutral is acceptable in the lifted foot, but mandatory for the supporting foot in both demi and full pointe.

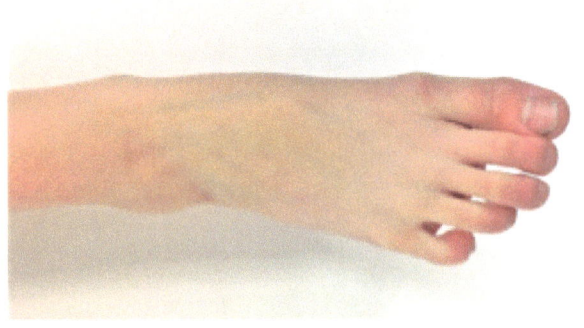

### A Flared Foot

Flaring is beautiful in the working foot and creates a lovely line, yet must not be used on the supporting foot as it rolls the weight of the body over the side of the big toe.

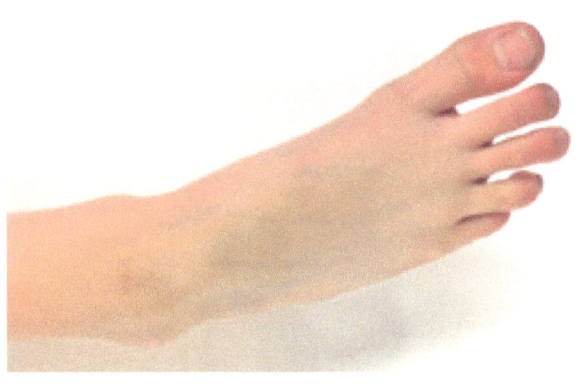

### A Sickled Foot

This is an unacceptable way of pointing in ballet. Though rarely seen in dancers other than beginners, it can show up through the lifted foot in retiré if it's allowed to rest on the knee, and when pointing derrière.

# FOOT Placement

*Using your feet correctly is mandatory for building and maintaining a proper foundation for pointe work.*

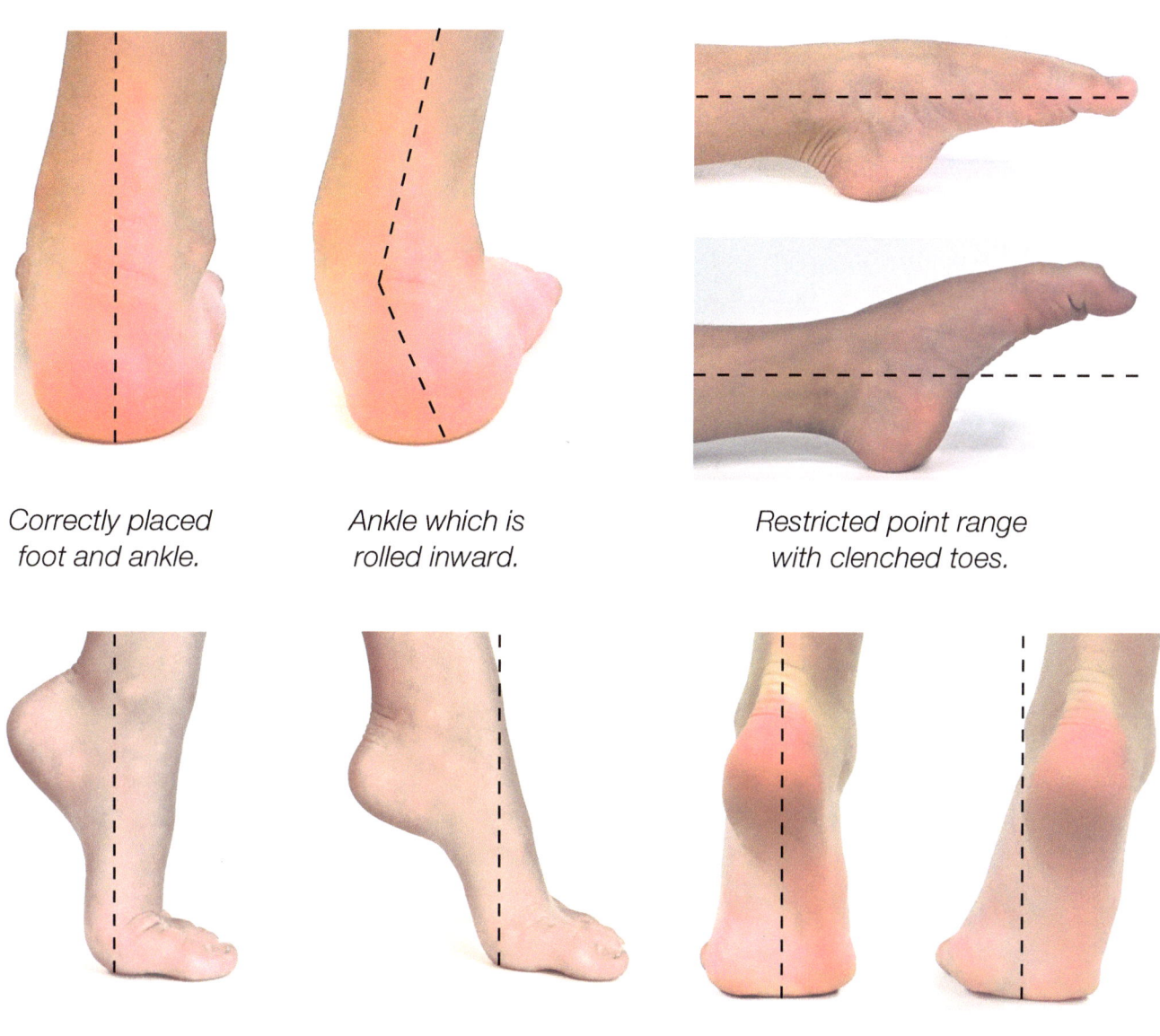

Correctly placed foot and ankle.

Ankle which is rolled inward.

Restricted point range with clenched toes.

Acceptable height on elevé with ankle over the ball of the foot.

Unacceptable height with ankle not over the ball of the foot.

Weight placed between big and 2nd toes.

Rolling outward onto the little toe.

# ABOUT The Winged Scapula

## What Causes Protruding Shoulder Blades?

Several muscles are attached to the shoulder blade which are used for its stabilization. If these muscles are not strong enough to hold the shoulder blades in their correct position against the ribs, the edge of the scapula will protrude or push outward. This can affect normal movements like lifting, pulling, pushing or throwing. Protruding shoulder blades are a common condition linked with poor posture and is generally ignored. In dance, however, it is not only unattractive but a posture problem which must not be ignored. Dancers can correct their protruding shoulder blades by learning to maintain proper posture and by strengthening the muscles which hold their scapulas in place - primarily the serratus anterior.

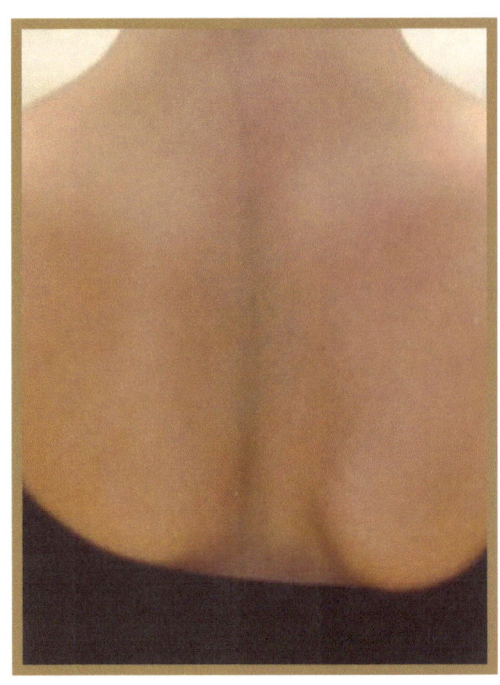

## The Scapula and Serratus Anterior

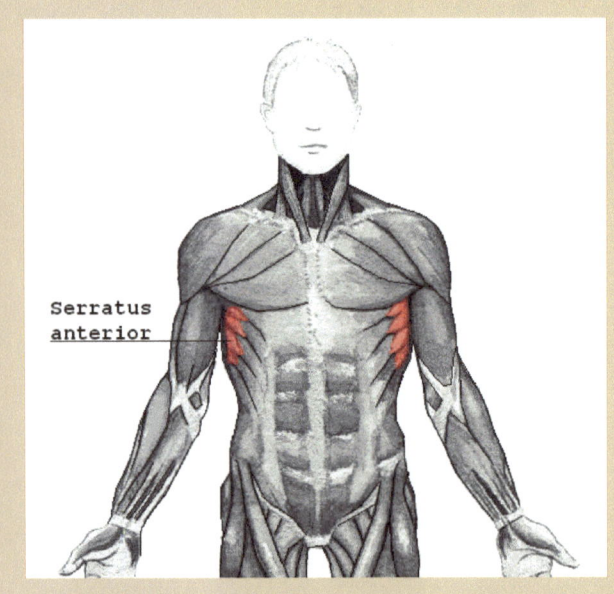

The largest, most complex part of the shoulder, the scapula attaches to many muscles allowing the arm to have a wide range of motion and still stay stabilized.

The serratus anterior is a large, wide muscle that attaches to 8 or 9 ribs and inserts into the inner border of the scapula. It holds the scapula flat against the ribs preventing winging.

# BACK AND SHOULDER Series

**Purpose:** Strengthens back and shoulder muscles to flatten shoulder blades.

## Pull Down and Back with Theraband

*Pull elbows down from shoulder blades in 5 counts. Hold 5 and return in 5. Do 10 - 15x.*

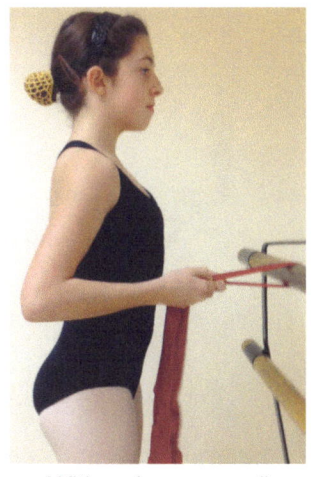

*With palms up. pull arms back from below shoulder blades in 5 counts. Hold 5 and return in 5. Do 10x.*

### 4 Count Shoulder Blade Exercise

Place your arms in 2nd with palms up. MOVE ONLY YOUR SHOULDER BLADES in this exercise.

#1 = Pinch shoulder blades together.

#2 = Lift shoulders blades up.

#3 = Reach shoulder blades out as far as possible.

#4 = Press shoulder blades down.

## The Serratus Anterior Press

Lie on the floor on your back with knees bent. Hold a weight in R hand and lift to ceiling. Place the L hand behind R elbow, holding it straight. Reach the raised arm upward, from under your shoulder. Return by actively pulling downward through the shoulder blade. Do 10x and repeat with other arm.

## Beginning/Advanced Breast Stroke

**Beginning:** On floor with no weights.
**Advanced:** Balance on exercise ball with weights.
- Preparation: Arms in 2nd, lift arms, chest, and head up, breathing in.
- Pose #1: Bend elbows bringing hands toward shoulders.
- Pose #2: Reach arms forward, lower head, tighten core and press your shoulder blades downward as you breathe out.
- Return: Breathe in opening arms to 2nd and lift back to starting position. Repeat - Do 10x.

*In 2nd move to pose #1 on count 1.*

*Reach forward to pose 2 on count 2. Hold 3 and return to 2nd on count 4.*

# ALIGNMENT   The Foundation of Dance

**Purpose:** All balanced movements extend from neutral.

### Technique

**1. Feet in 1st:** Weight equally divided between both feet on big toes, little toes and heels.

**2. Ankles:** lifted and not rolling either in or out.

**3. Legs:** Turned out from the hips with stretched knees (not pushing back or relaxing forward).

**4. Hips:** Pulled up through the core with tailbone reaching to floor not tucked under.

**5. Ribs:** Held in and lifted.

**6. Shoulders:** Carried over crest of hip bones with chest lifted and shoulder blades flat against ribs.

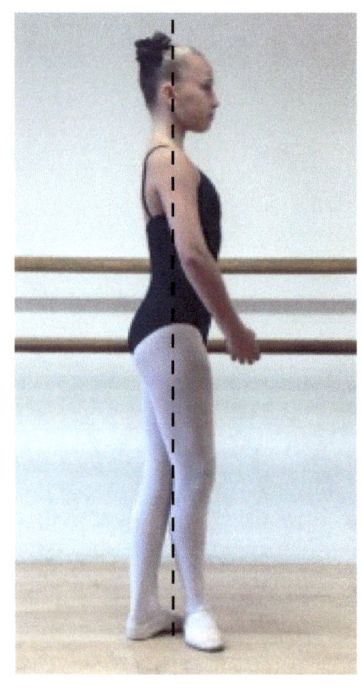

*A well-placed body centered, pulled up and held yet not stiff.*

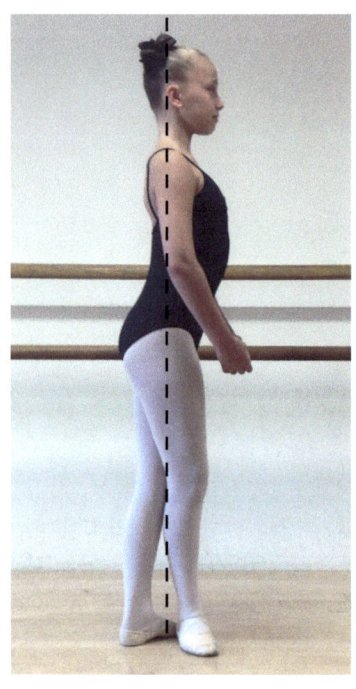

*With ribs and shoulders forward the hips move back.*

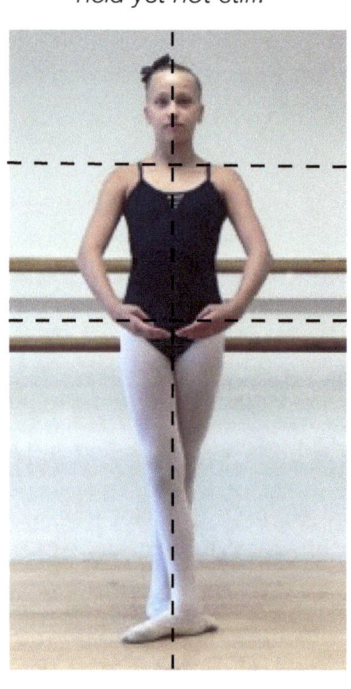

*Upper torso carried over top of hip bones, elbows in front of body and knees stretched.*

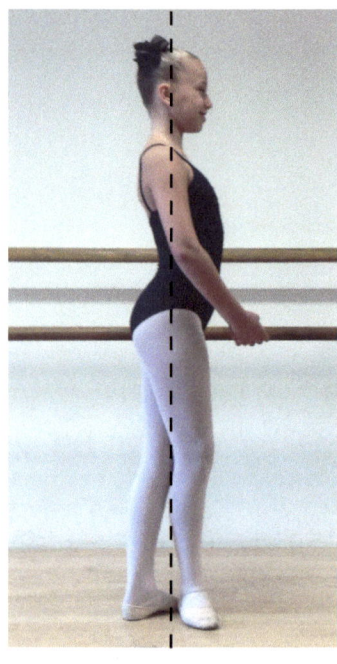

*Core released and hips tilted to create a sway back posture.*

# FINDING Neutral

**Purpose:** To learn the feeling of neutral and successfully return.

### Correcting Ribs Out

**Standing with ribs out is generally an awareness problem.**

**Exercise:** Place one hand on the top of your chest and the other just below the sternum arch. Breathe out pressing your ribs in. Hold that position and breathe in expanding your ribs to the side and lifting your chest. Now breathe out keeping your chest against your upper hand. Continue for 20 breaths.

### Correcting Sway Back

**Strengthening your core muscles and learning to keep them engaged as well as lengthening your body will correct sway back.**

**Exercise:** Place one hand on your belly button and the other behind your back. Breathe in lifting your chest without pressing your spine against your back hand. Breathe out without changing position. Hold this position for 20 breaths.

*For additional core strengthening exercises see "Core and Back" chapter 7.*

## Faulty Postures

### Ribs Out

Holding the ribcage out in front takes the shoulders forward as well. The hips are forced to shift back to counter-balance forcing the body out of alignment along its axis.

It is extremely important that posture corrections be made and practiced throughout each class.

### Sway Back

Relaxing through the core allows the pelvis to tilt forward and the spine to curve. With this, the shoulders fall back, elbows drop in, the neck is pressed forward and the chin drops.

# ALIGNMENT While Standing in Retiré

### Hip Squareness

Think of squareness as the relationship between your shoulders, hips, and the floor. Hips and shoulders stay held, like boxes stacked upon each other sitting squarely on the floor. One box doesn't lift, tilt, or twist from the other, and both don't tilt from the floor.

*Correct hips and shoulders held square and weight 60% on the ball of the foot.*

### Exploring balancing dynamics of 1st vs. 5th

- Stand in first, in front of a mirror.
- Without adjusting your weight, lift one foot to retiré. You will always fall toward your raised leg.
- Now, stand in fifth. Feel your standing foot's weight placement (60% on your ball and 40% on your heel) as you lift one foot into retiré. This position is easily balanced as 5th naturally places your hips for an aligned single leg stand.
- Now shift your weight back on your heel and see what happens.

### Exploring weight changing adjustments

programs your brain with the knowledge it needs to make accurate changes automatically while you dance.

**Incorrect**
*Hip raised a little with upper body tilted to compensate. Very little turnout elbows in front of body and knees stretched.*

**Incorrect**
*Hip lifted and pulled back, core released, shoulders in front of center, weight back on heel and turnout not held.*

# MAINTAINING NEUTRAL
## Alignment While in Elevé Retiré

### Exploring the balancing dynamics in elevé

- Stand in 5th, in front of a mirror.
- Raise one foot to retiré, well turned out.
- Keep hips square by pressing in and down through the piriformis area.
- Check your core's squareness in the mirror.
- Press your heel just off the floor and return maintaining placement.
- Raise your heel higher, balance 3 counts and lower without falling or losing control.
- Now, rise to full demi-pointe, balance 3 counts and lower smoothly to your well-placed starting position.

Perfecting the above exercise develops placement skills for pirouettes.

### Technique

**1. Supporting leg:** Weight carried between big and second toes with knee straight and turned out.

**2. Raised leg:** Hips stay in neutral as the knee lifts quickly in turnout with well pointed foot (not sickled).

**3. Torso:** hips and shoulders held in alignment.

**4. Arms, neck and head:** Held but not tense.

**Incorrect**
*Hip raised, body tilted, heel not to full demi-pointe.*

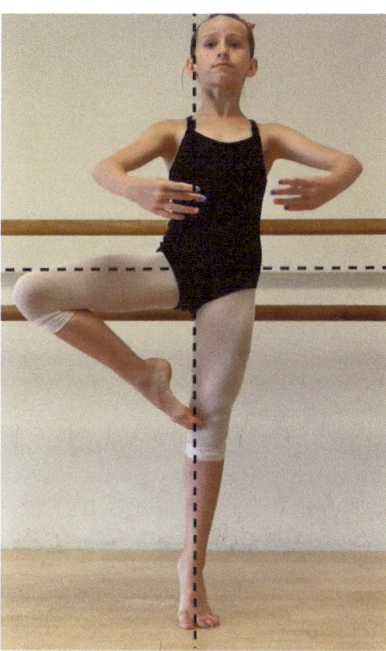

**Incorrect**
*Very little turnout and arms not centered.*

*Well-placed elevé retiré (arms need centering).*

# The HEAD AND NECK Series

**Purpose:** To find neutral head placement and strengthen neck muscles.

**Head Lowered**

### 5 Positions of the Head
There are five primary positions of the head:
1. neutral or erect, 2. turned, 3. raised, 4. lowered and 5. inclined. Every other head position is a combination of two or more of these positions. Jutting the head forward is a placement error and not a position in ballet.

*NOTE: Head placement seems easy, but errors often show up, especially when spotting. If your head raises, lowers or inclines as you spot, your turn will be thrown off center.*

### Isotonic Neck Strengthening - Do 10x each

*With hands resisting, slowly tilt head back 1 inch. Hold 6 counts. Return to neutral.*

*Press hand to R side of head. Slowly tilt into hand. Return to neutral and repeat.*

*For resistance, place hands on forehead and slowly lower chin. Hold 6 cnts. Return to neutral. Do 10x*

### Finding Neutral

*Begin in Neutral - chin level, held below the nose. Turn head R, center, L.*

*Raise chin, return to neutral, then lower chin and return.*

*Incline head R and return to neutral. Repeat L.*

*Press chin forward, return to neutral, back and return to neutral.*

**NOTE:**

All persistent problems or strong pain needs to be seen by your doctor and physical therapist for rehabilitation. The material contained in this book is strictly for developing strong ballet technique and a general knowledge for the care and workings of your body.

# ASSESSMENTS #1 - #4

### #1 - Alignment in 1st     #2 - Alignment in Demi-Plié

**Purpose:** To assess a dancer's alignment, discover faulty technique, and make necessary corrections.

| **Alignment Errors:** | **Correcting Errors:** |
|---|---|
| • rolled ankles and knees.... | • strengthen foot and ankle muscles |
| • lack of turnout................. | • turnout stretches and strengthening |
| • swayed back.................... | • core awareness and strengthening |
| • ribs held out..................... | • placement and lengthening spine |
| • winged shoulder blades.... | • shoulder blade exercises |
| • protruding chin................. | • head/neck exercises/awareness |
| • elbows drop in.................. | • placement awareness |
| • knees not straight............. | • pull up through legs/awareness |
| • knees not over toes when in plié...................... | • work on placement and turnout |

### #3 and #4 - Demi-Plié Depth

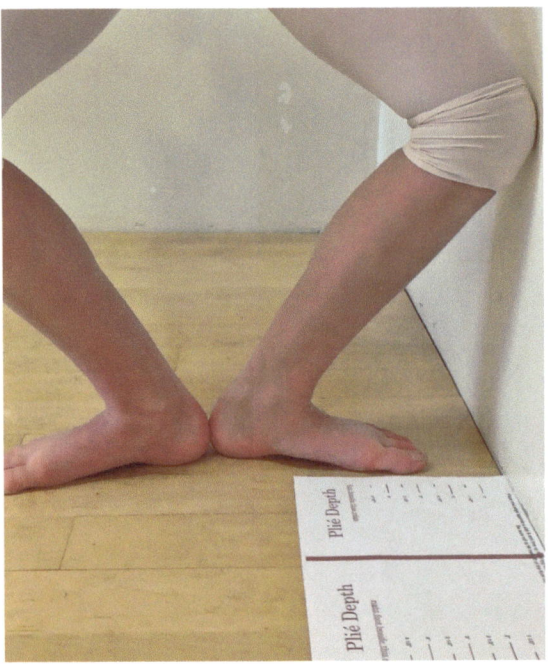

**Purpose:** To make certain the depth of your demi-plié reaches 2 1/2" to 4 1/2" (depending on your height) and is equal on both legs.

**NOTE:** Chart is located in back of "To the Pointe Workbook."

**Deepening Your Demi-Plié:** Do calf stretches holding 20 counts. Do 10x/day. A shallow demi-plié depth, forces heels to pop up, jumps to lack power and landings to lack cushion. Unequal depth creates imbalance. Do twice as many calf stretches on restricted leg.

# ALIGNMENT AND PLIÉ DEPTH
## Assessments #1 - #4

| ASSESSMENTS | REQUIREMENTS TO PASS |
| --- | --- |
| **#1 - Standing Posture in 1st** | A. Head erect with chin parallel to floor and neck stretched long away from shoulders.<br>B. Shoulder blades held flat against back and not protruding. Shoulders held open, level and over top of pelvic bones.<br>C. Back lengthened, with slight curve in small of back.<br>D. Ribs held in and up. Breathing is from side and top of ribs.<br>E. Core engaged lifting inward and upward.<br>F. Maintain the largest turnout possible.<br>G. Knees held in neutral - not hypo. or hyperextended.<br>H. Feet and ankles correctly held on balancing points - not rolling in nor out. |
| **#2 - Demi-Plié Alignment in 5th** | Posture held as above in demi-plié with knees over toes (further plié information in Knees and Legs chapter). |
| **#3 and #4 - Plié Depth** | In 1st, 2 1/2" to 4 1/2" (depending on your height) from a wall. Demi-plié until your knee touches the wall. Both knees need to show the same depth of plié. See measurement chart in back of workbook. |

# PAIN
## Good Pain vs. Bad Pain

As you progress toward pointe, you will increase your hours of training and will begin extending the difficulty of your work. You also need to learn more about your body and begin understanding 'good pain' vs. 'bad pain.' There IS a difference between the sensations of a muscle which has worked hard (after exercise muscle soreness) and the overloaded and painful feeling of an injury. Some students complain at the slightest bit of discomfort, while others will never complain despite the most intense pain.

Dancers, however, need to speak freely about what they are feeling in their body and consult a teacher if they are concerned about one area being always 'sore.' Bad pain is your body telling you that something is wrong and needs to be addressed, perhaps even seen by a doctor. Any persisting sharp pain, a pain inside the foot, deep inside the hip, or a radiating pain should be checked by a medical professional. Don't try to work through it.

The good pain of sore muscles is part of the strengthening process and will last around 48 hours. Another good pain is that of returning to normal following a healed injury.

### "I KNOW IT HURTS," THE DOCTOR SAID, "BUT YOU'VE GOT TO KEEP WALKING THROUGH IT."

This quote is from a discussion between a doctor and his patient following a broken foot bone. It's the only way for muscles to rebuild and connective tissue to become unstuck and re-pattern itself back to something more functional.

Dancers must develop an instinct - a gut feeling - about their own body. Trust it, and listen to it. Then, you can determine if a pain is something that can be worked through or something that needs attention.

*"Injuries can occur from accidents, but more often, are the result of faulty form."*
Dancing Without Danger

# 3 DANGERS WHICH CAN LEAD TO INJURY

## FOCUS - INADEQUATE STRENGTH - BODY LIMITS

**Focus** or rather the lack of focus can cause a dancer to misjudge a landing or movement causing loss of control and injury.

**Inadequate Strength** and flexibility limits a dancer's scope of ability. Pushing beyond abilities can lead to injury.

**Body Limits** exist in everyone and change through time. It is important to understand your own body and its current personal limits. When you're overly fatigued, dance with caution. If your legs start shaking, know that they have reached their limit and could fail. This is not to say you should stop and sit down. Just use caution especially during leaps and turns.

## 5 SIGNS OF TROUBLE

| | |
|---|---|
| **1. Growth Spurts** | They diminish a dancer's strength, balance and coordination. |
| **2. Faulty Landings** | Injuries can occur from failure to control a landing (toe, ball, heel, plié) or failing out of a turn. Incorrect knee/ankle placement (rolling in). Inadequate plié depth. |
| **3. Holding Tension** | Locking the pelvis under compromises movement flow. Rigid upper body causes neck and shoulder problems. |
| **4. Lack of Control** | Failure to use muscles, which hold your placement, opens you to injury. Particularly in the core, which will leave you vulnerable to back injuries. |
| **5. Tight rib cage** | The ribcage is designed to move in all directions, and dancers, though holding ribs in and lifted, must not allow them to become rigid. |

# Chapter 2

# ASSESSMENTS 5 - 8

## *Feet and Ankles*

Dancers' feet must be resilient to the constant, repetitive demands of ballet. They must provide fantastic control and support for each movement their body makes. This is why having strong foot muscles has such a tremendous effect on the long-term health of dancers' feet, the development of their bones, their balancing skills, and their ability to prevent injuries—especially overuse injuries in the tendons and muscles of the lower legs.

# SUMMARY
## *Chapter 2*
# FEET AND ANKLES

Dancers' feet must be supple and strong - very strong. In order to create these wonderful feet, students must incorporate foot strengthening exercises throughout their day as well as develop the habit of using their feet fully in all dance classes.

## STRENGTHENING YOUR FEET and ROLLING ANKLES:

Exercises to strengthen those small muscles beneath your feet like Doming, Toe Swapping, Toe Spread or Metatarsal Press can be done in your street shoes or barefoot, at school, during meals, seated or standing, anytime you remember. Do them often (20x/day).

## STRENGTHENING YOUR ANKLES:

Exercises strengthening the ankles, lower leg and foot muscles like Double or Single elevés on a Step, The Flair or Sickle should be practiced often but remember to do them slowly.

## INCREASING YOUR POINT RANGE:

### Stretching Out Restricted Toes:

To extend a restricted big toe as well as clenched or clawed toes, incorporate Up the Wall Toe Stretches as well as Standing or Seated Beneath the Toe Stretches.

### Stretching Out The Front Of Your Ankles:

Do the Kneeling, Seated or Standing Ankle Stretches throughout your day. The Seated Ankle Stretch can even be done in school while at your desk. Have a friend press your feet down but don't forget to continually strengthen those little muscles beneath your feet so they can point your foot.

## THE FLICKING TENDONS NEMESIS:

The danger in using the wrong muscles to hold your instep strong while balancing is in causing overuse injuries in the lower leg. Muscles within your foot (intrinsic) should be made strong enough to hold your instep steady and not need to enlist the help of the lower leg muscles (extrinsic).

# ANATOMY of the Foot

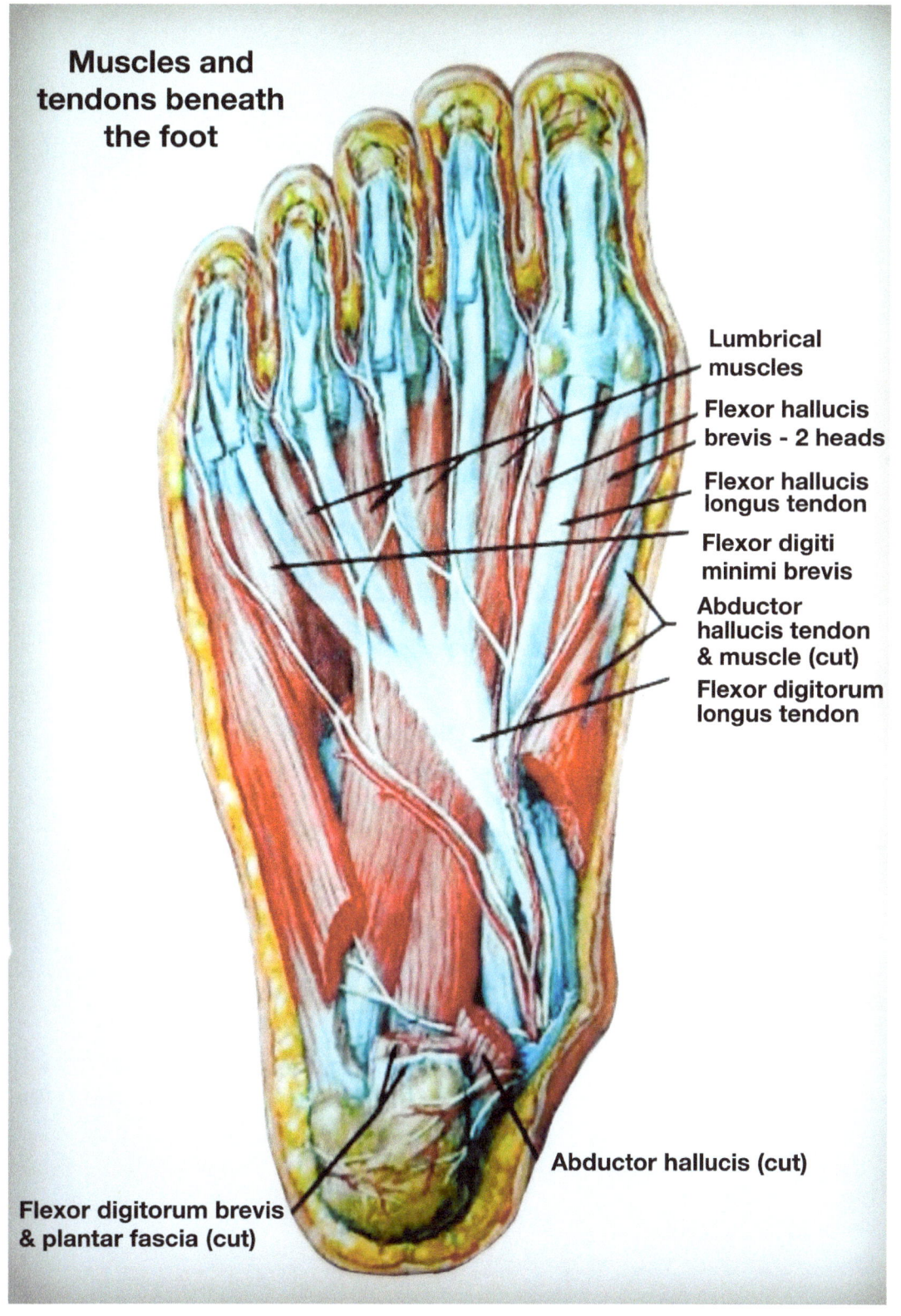

# OUR FANTASTIC Feet

*Our Fantastic Feet are our foundation. Their strength and stability are mandatory for dancers. They bear our weight, propel us in all directions, and balance our entire body.*

## THE HUMAN FOOT IS MADE OF:
### 26 bones - 33 joints - and more than 100 muscles, tendons and ligaments.

## *Muscles and Tendons Controlling Our Feet*

### INTRINSIC VS. EXTRINSIC

**INTRINSIC** - located within the foot • **EXTRINSIC** - located in the lower leg

**Intrinsic muscles** are small. Some are very small, and they need to be strong to help us do all that we want to do in dance.

**Extrinsic muscles** are much larger making it easier to take over the job of the intrinsic muscles. This, however, leaves them vulnerable to overuse injuries as well as creating movements we don't want - like clawed toes.

### MOVING THE BIG TOE

**The Flexor Hallucis Brevis** *(2 headed muscle shown second from top in foot picture)* an intrinsic muscle (within the foot) flexes the big toe and is strengthened by doing the big toe exercise.

**The Flexor Hallucis Longus Tendon** *(shown third from top)* extrinsically flexes the big toe through its muscle in the lower leg. Because it controls the big toe from outside the foot it is an extrinsic muscle.

**The Abductor Hallucis Tendon and Muscle** *(shown second from bottom)* are intrinsic and flair the big toe outward.

**The Extensor Hallucis Longus Tendon** *(not shown)* attaches to its muscle in front of the shin and lifts the big toe.

# MOVING THE SMALL TOES

**The Lumbricals** (first listed in "Foot Anatomy" chart) and the **Interosseous** (3 very small muscles which lie below the lumbricals - not shown) are intrinsic muscles which control the correctly pointed foot. They are strengthened through articulated tendus and the doming series of exercises. Strengthening these muscles eases the load placed on the lower leg (extrinsic) muscles when dancing.

**The Flexor Digitorum Brevis** (cut) is the outermost muscle moving the little toes.

**The Flexor Digitorum Longus Tendon** (shown below on right) connects to its muscle extrinsically located beneath the calf and curls the toes under.

**The Extensor Digitorum Longus Tendon** (shown below on left) is located on the top of the foot. It pulls the toes upward.

## EXTRINSIC TOE MUSCLES

### Extensor Digitorum Longus
Its tendons attach to the top of your toes pulling them upward. When balancing on one foot, this is one of the tendons which can flick off and on attempting to hold your balance from the top of your foot.

### CLENCHED OR CLAWED TOES
When your toes are clawed or clenched, it's because you're grabbing with the *extrinsic* muscles for balance or pointing. Strengthen your *intrinsic* muscles and learn to stretch your toes.

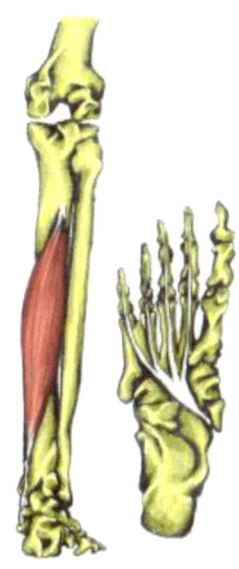

**Flexor Digitorum Longus**
These tendons attach to the bottom of the toes and grips them downward.

*NOTE: A beautifully pointed foot uses your calf muscles to point your ankle and your intrinsic foot muscles to arch your foot and point your toes.*

# THE **THREE ARCHES** OF OUR FEET

- **The Medial Arch:** the arch we know best - our instep - runs from our big toe to the heel on the inside of our foot.

- **The Transverse Arch:** runs perpendicular to our instep across our metatarsal bones.

- **The Lateral Arch:** running down the outside of our foot parallel to our instep.

*Arches are essential for movement, supporting our weight, and providing our foot with the flexibility it needs for shock absorption.*

## THE HEIGHTS OF OUR ARCHES

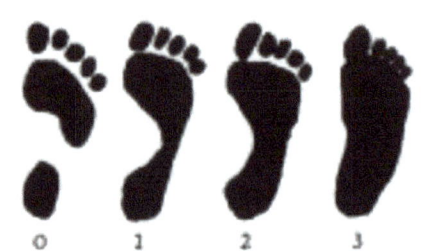

0 = very high arch   1 = a high arch
2 = neutral foot     3 = flat foot

#0 - Dancers with high arches tend toward weak feet and can be knock-kneed with rolling ankles.

#1- They must to work on strengthening the muscles under the foot to support this large instep.

#2- A good shock-absorbing arch.

#3- Flat feet are dangerous because they provide very little shock absorption, and excessive stretching of the foot's plantar fascia can cause it to tear.

## FOOT SHAPES

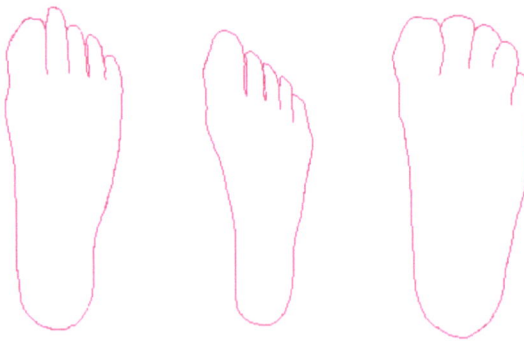

**GREEK FOOT**

The second toe is longer.

**EGYPTIAN FOOT**

The big toe is longer.
It is most common.

**PEASANT OR GISELLE FOOT**

The first three toes are close to the same length.

# MASTERING Tendu

*Tendu to stretch: a primary building block of ballet. It is often misunderstood and poorly executed.*

## Components of a Correctly Executed Tendu

1. **Master core control:** Your tendu begins by engaging core as well as relying on your deep back and core stability muscles.

2. **Be continually aware of your standing leg's turnout muscles and build up their endurance:** Without contracting the gluteals, contract the quadratus femoris (the lowest muscle in the piriformis group). It is the best muscle to hold turnout in your standing leg.

3. **Lift up through the supporting leg and distribute foot weight correctly (60/40):**

   *NOTE: Knees that are hyper- or hypoextended have difficulty with control when moving from two feet to one - as in tendu. Learn to hold your knees in neutral yet not too tense.*

   Begin in 5th with your weight distributed equally on both feet in the "tripod stand." Engage your core and turnout muscles in both legs and lift up out of your hips.

4. **Articulated tendu:** Press your working heel forward and shift an additional 10% more weight onto the ball of your supporting foot. Keep your working heel on the floor as long as possible without changing your alignment. Stretch to the ball of that foot keeping your toes long. Not allowing your toes to leave the floor, point them long (avoid clawing or clenching). Return with the little toe leading back and pressing your heel down as soon as possible. (Don't change the position of your body - only the leg moves) Return to your beginning position by squeezing the thighs together and not allowing your knee to bend. When doing tendus derrière, begin by first moving your little toe, then heel, stretch your leg out to the ball and finally point the toes.

5. **Additional movements:** When you think of it, this same movement is used when taking off or landing a jump or rolling up or down en pointe. The smoothness, control, and safety achieved when landing **toe, ball, heel, plié** is a mandatory element in ballet as well as in pointe work.

# DOMING Series

**Purpose:** For building strength and developing awareness in the small muscles within your feet and toes. Strong foot muscles are mandatory for raising and lowering en pointe, balancing, and easing the load placed on extrinsic foot muscles.

## Technique

1. When Doming, press heel and all toes equally downward while lifting your instep as high as possible.

   A. Do not clench or claw your toes as this uses the wrong muscles (extrinsic).

   B. Keep ankles straight and not rolling in or out.

2. In Caterpillar, after each move, form a high dome with toes stretched long before releasing.

**DO AS OFTEN AS POSSIBLE THROUGHOUT YOUR DAY.**

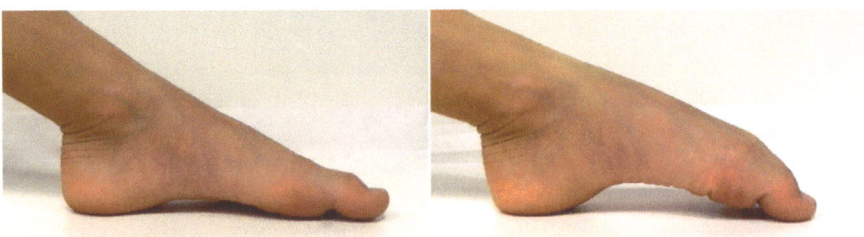

**Doming:** With your foot in the tripod stand, press your arches as high as possible without clenching or clawing your toes. Hold 10 counts. Do 20x on each foot, 5x a day.

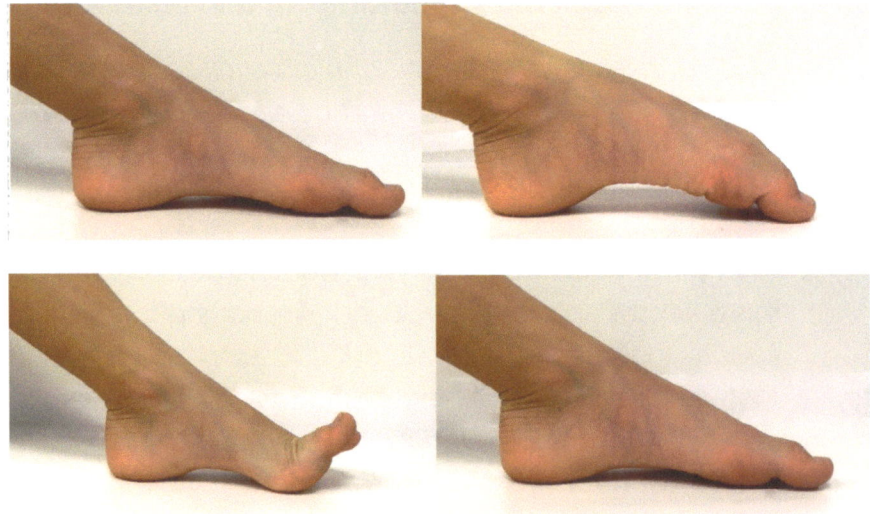

**Caterpillar:** With your foot in tripod stand, press your arches as high as possible to form a dome as above. Lift your toes and move the ball of your foot forward then pull your heel forward to form your next dome. Continue walking your foot forward until you can go no further. Reverse traveling backward.

# ELEVÉ Series

**Purpose:** For strength and control of the muscles within your feet, ankles, and calf.

## Double Leg Elevé on a Step

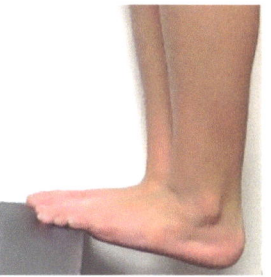

Stand on the ball of your foot on a step in parallel with heels off the edge. Lower heels as low as possible. Slowly elevé 5 counts to full demi-pointe, and lower 5 counts. Do 10x 3x/day.

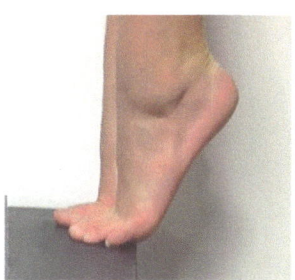

## Single Leg Elevé on a Step

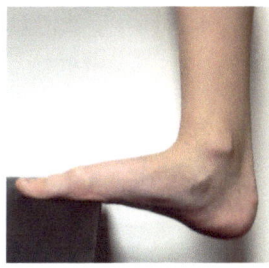

Repeat as above on one foot. Be sure to rise to the highest demi-pointe you can reach and don't rush your counts. Do 5x on each leg 3x/day.

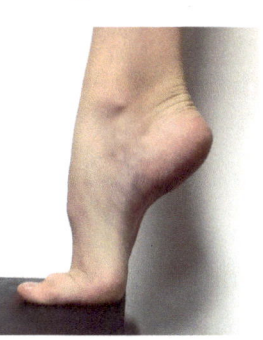

## Seated Elevé

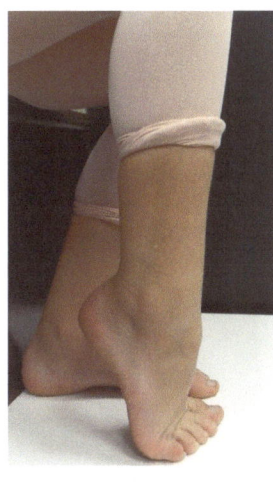

Sitting with feet on floor in parallel, lean forward resting your elbows on one knee. Press that heel upward as high as possible in 5 counts. Then, lower 5 counts. Do 5x/foot 3x/day. Repeat on other foot. When mastered, press to full pointe.

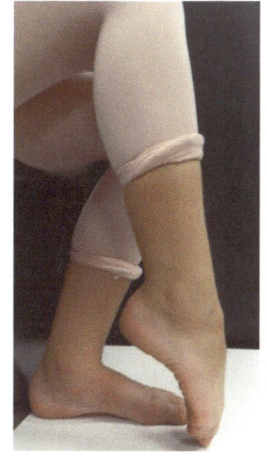

### Technique

1. Keep toes long and relaxed throughout these exercises.

2. Lower your heel as far below the step as possible for a good calf stretch.

3. Make sure your weight is carried between big toe and second toe.

4. Keep your elevé slow and smooth. Return in the same way.

5. Whatever you hold for balance, hold it lightly and don't pull.

**ALWAYS STRETCH YOUR CALVES AFTER ELEVÉ AND SAUTÉ EXERCISES.**

# MORE EXERCISES FOR Foot Muscles

**Don't neglect the small muscles in your foot,
they are extremely important for pointe work.**

**Articulated Tendu (as explained on page 43).**

*Do Articulated Tendus every time you perform tendus in class.*

### Ball Grab
Standing or seated with a tennis ball under one foot: Attempt to pick up the ball by using only the bottom of your foot. This can also be done with your toes picking up a golf ball. Be sure to use only your intrinsic muscles.

### Ball Stand
Stand on a soccer-sized ball with both feet for as long as possible. At first, barefoot. Then with socks. Finally, with ballet shoes.

### Toe Swapping
Seated on the floor or in a chair with your feet flat on the floor: Lift the big toe up then switch, lifting the little toes up then moving the big toe down. Be sure your metatarsal bones don't lift off the floor.

### Piano Toes
Similar to toe swapping. Lift toes up one at a time and lower one at a time as though playing the piano. Again, keep the ball of your foot on the floor.

### Ball Rolls
Roll a golf ball, tube or glass bottle beneath your foot. Move it all around. This massages the bottom of your foot releasing tension and can have spectacular results with the curve of your arch.

### Cat's Paw

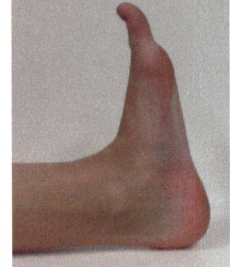
*Begin seated w/ legs straight and your feet flexed.*

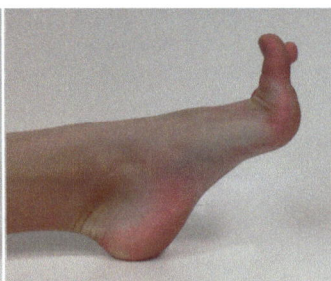
*Press through the ball of your foot toward the floor.*

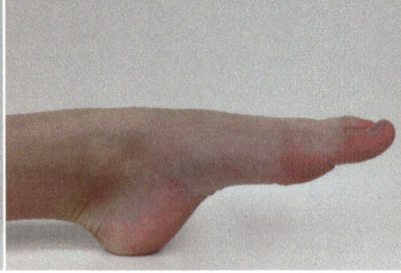
*Press through the point of your toes.*

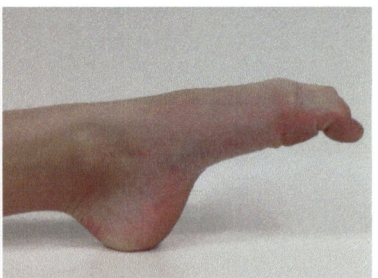
*Point toes down from the ball as you lift your foot to repeat.*

# YOUR RESTRICTED Pointe Range

There are two reasons your feet are unable to reach the full elevé height necessary for pointe work.

1. Lack of flexibility in ankle or big toe.
2. Lack of foot strength.

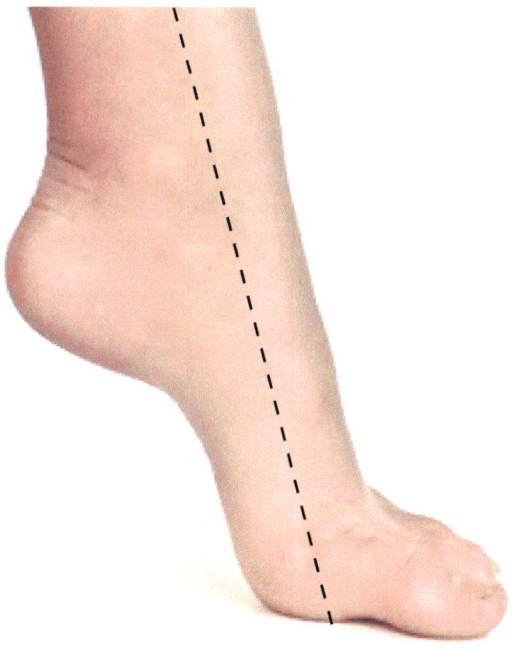

*Insufficient height for pointe*

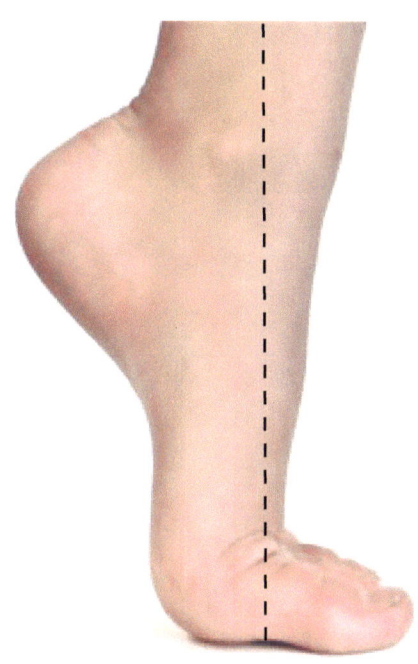

*Sufficient height for pointe*

## Why Feet Can't Reach Their Needed Pointe Range

**Lack of Flexibility**

Some feet are tightly put together in front of the ankle and need gentle but consistent stretching to achieve a sufficient range for pointe work. Elevé pointe range can also be limited by a restricted big toe (usually a tight flexor hallucis brevis) and can be remedied through massage and stretching.

**Lack of Strength**

Other dancers have foot flexibility but lack sufficient strength in their feet to reach the range necessary for pointe work. If this is your situation, lots of foot strengthening exercises are needed to achieve your goal.

# Increasing Your POINTE RANGE

Be sure your heel is held directly behind your toes and rolls neither in nor out (no pain should be felt behind the ankle).

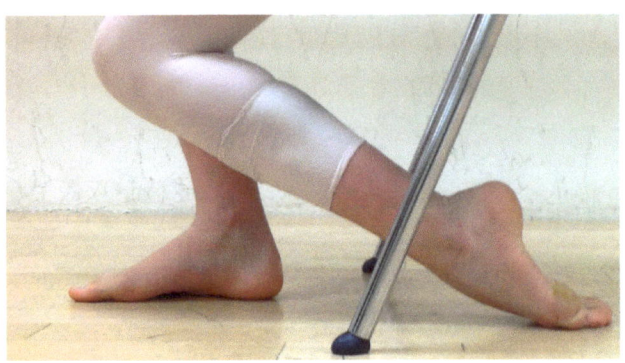
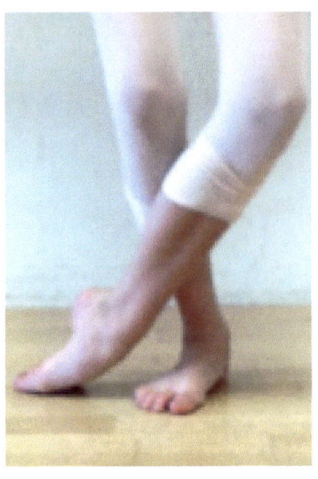

**Kneeling Pointe Stretch**
*Slowly lift your knee off the floor, hold for 30 sec. Return and repeat.*

**Seated Pointe Stretch**
*Slowly press weight onto the top of your arch. Make sure you are pressing on top of your arch—not your toes. Hold for 30 sec.*

**Standing Pointe Stretch**
*With the back leg touching the front, slowly plié. Hold for 30 sec.*

Do any pointe stretch (mix and match) a minimum of 5x/day.

**Plié in elevé:** In 6th position (parallel 1st), elevé 4 counts as high as possible. Plié forward 4 counts pressing your heels forward as far as possible. Straighten your knees 4 counts trying to keep your heels forward. Lower 4 counts to the floor. Don't clench or claw.

## Essential Tests to Pass Before Pointe

**Seated Pointe Range**
This is a non-weight-bearing test which determines if a dancer's pointe range is sufficient for pointe work. If limited, foot and ankle flexibility can be extended through stretching, shown above, though it takes time and consistency.

**Elevé Pointe Range**
The elevé pointe range test is a weight-bearing test to determine a dancer's full demi-pointe range. If you lack the needed strength, lots of foot strengthening exercises are in order. If stiffness is the issue, perform lots of stretching. As above, these concerns can be improved with a daily exercise program.

# ABOUT A STIFF Big Toe

## Hallux Limitus:

This is a condition characterized by restricted movement in the big toe, which may or may not be accompanied by pain. Full demi-pointe forms a 90° angle from the floor up through the center of the big toe's metatarsal bone to the center of the ankle bone. The knee must remain straight and the toes long. A stiff big toe will prevent this and can cause sickling onto the little toe.

A stiff big toe can be caused by the actual bones of the foot, as in a raised first metatarsal bone found in dancers having flat feet, or with an extra long second metatarsal bone where the second toe is longer than the big toe. It can also be caused from bone spurs in older people. Sometimes the limitation is due to tightness in the flexor hallucis longus or brevis.

## Mobilization Exercises for Big Toe:

Start seated and stabilize your foot by holding it firmly with one hand. Then grasp your big toe between the thumb and index finger with the other hand and do the following exercises 4 to 6x/day:

1. **Extensions:** Pull the big toe out and away from the metatarsal bone.

2. **Rotations:** Roll the big toe from side to side.

3. **Gliding:** Slide the big toe sideways, outward and inward from the metatarsal bone. Slide the big toe up and down from the metatarsal bone.

4. **Opening and Closing:** Press the top of the big toe inward then outward.

**Very little movement is necessary, and each movement should be slow and deliberate.**

### Now that you have warmed up your big toe, try exercises on page 51:

1. The standing or seated toe stretch.
2. Up the wall toe stretch.

# ABOUT CLAWED and Clenched Toes

## The "Clawed and Clenched Toe" Phenomenon!

Some dancers feel that it is almost impossible to keep their toes lengthened when pointing; however, it can be mastered. If your toes have been contracted for some time, the soft tissues under them may need some TLC!! Gently massage beneath the toes with your fingers (this is really good after giving your feet a warm foot bath for at least 10 minutes to soften the tissues). Slowly stretch each toe and assess its full range. You may be quite surprised at how much range you actually do have! "If the toes are limited in their range, do not despair! Our bodies are undergoing constant change and while this does slow down a little as we age, there is always potential to change the way things are," writes Lisa Howell.

## Stretching and Massage:

To relax and lengthen the area under your toes do any, or all, of the stretches shown on the next page. In doing these stretches, you will feel the fascia and tendons stretching beneath your toes. These stretches can feel sharp, but should not be painful.

Lisa also said, "While you need mobility in the under surface of your toes, you also need some mobility on the top of the toes. Many dancers who are 'clawing' initially have very tight structures over their 'knucklebones,' and this makes it very difficult to point from the right area. Assess the mobility of each of your toe knuckles, both with the ankle flexed, and with it pointed. You will probably find that the clawing toes are restricted and will give a strong stretching feeling over the top part of the foot. Gentle massage in this area by massaging up between the toe bones combined with gentle stretching will really help open out this area."

When you have extended the range of motion in your toes, you will be able to do additional foot exercises correctly and more easily by not clawing. Doming, when properly done, for instance, helps you point from your knuckles and roll up from demi onto full pointe. Releasing clawed toes helps avoid overuse injuries to the muscles in the shin.

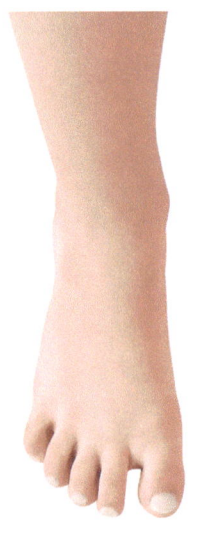  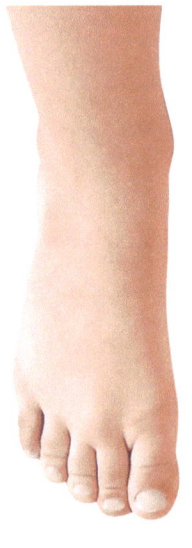  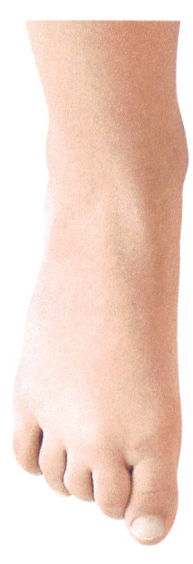

*Neutral*  *Clenched*  *Clawed*

# EXERCISES FOR CLENCHED and Clawed Toes

**Purpose:** To promote toe control and dexterity and lengthen the area beneath the toes.

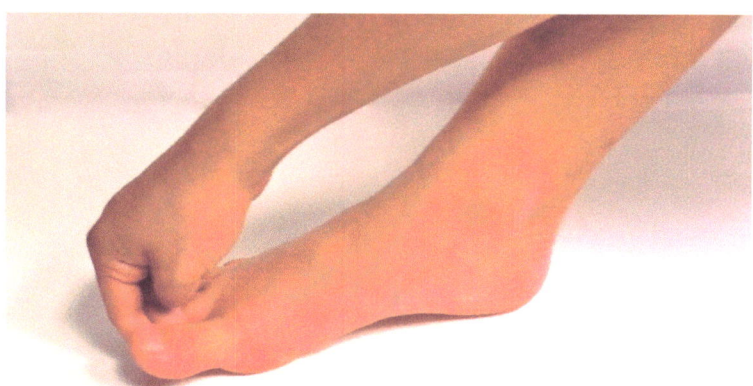

**Massage under the Toes**

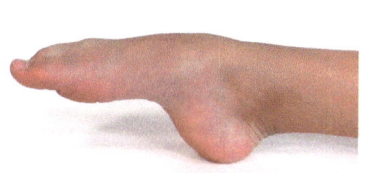 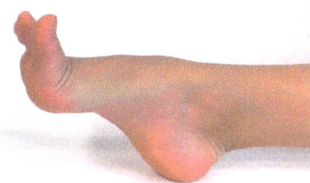

**Eyelashes**

With your heels on the floor, point your toes then pull your toes back as far as you can. Then point again as far as possible without curling them under. Do 20x 3x/day.

## Technique

**MASSAGE UNDER THE TOES**
Reach under each toe and rub the muscles out, stretching the toe long and releasing any held tension.

**EYELASHES**
This is a great exercise for those who need work on keeping their toes straight. It will take a lot of effort not to curl them under. If needed, use your fingers to hold them straight.

**TOE STRETCHES**
Keep the ball of your foot over its balancing point without rolling out or in. Keep your toes long and your heel directly behind your toes. Make sure your knees stay over your toes.

**ALSO ADD THE SOLIUS STRETCH (found in Knees and Legs chapter)**

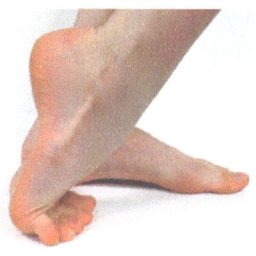

**Standing or Seated Toe Stretch**
In parallel with one foot back and your toes on the floor, plié pressing forward as far as you can. Hold 20 counts. Repeat.

**Up the Wall Toe Stretch**
Place your toes up a wall with the ball of your foot at the base of the wall and raise your heel. Hold 20 counts. Release and repeat.

**Blisters and Pointe Shoes**
Because blisters on the toe knuckles are caused from not stretching your toes long inside your pointe shoes, train your feet now to eliminate this problem.

**For Best Results**
1. Warm up your feet and lower leg muscles
2. Massage to release tension
3. Stretch

# **IS IT POSSIBLE** to Prevent Bunions?

The answer is still up in the air, but I know exercise, proper shoes, and correct technique certainly helps. We know that bunions are inherited, and the accepted cure for bunions today is surgery. The former, we have no control over and the latter, we want to avoid. So - what CAN we do to help?

First, become aware of your propensity for bunions. Should you find you're in the bunion group, there are wonderful tools like bunion splints, which you can wear at night (they keep your toes in a straight position), and jell spacers, which you can wear between your big toe and second toe during the day. Bunions and rolling ankles tend to go together, so an orthotic insert for your walking shoes (no flip flops) will place your foot in a corrected position while you are strengthening your feet. Now create your daily improvement program in your workbook with planned exercises for your toes, feet, and ankles as shown in this chapter.

There is much you can do in class for bunions. First, become very aware of any faulty technique you perform which forces your big toe inward. For example, in tendu derrière, don't rest your weight on the outside of your big toe because it forces it inward. Don't allow your ankle to roll in when standing or landing jumps - especially the back foot!!! Constantly be aware of your weight placement in class and don't allow your foot to roll off the little toe onto your bunion. Rolling ankles are especially hard on the big toe, forcing it to roll over and inward. Make sure the little toe and the back of your foot stay on the floor, your instep is pulled up with **EVERY PLIÉ YOU DO,** and **ALWAYS** open your knees over your toes in all plié movements. This is super important when landing in plié on one leg. Develop the habit of continually checking your plié placement. Diligence will soon establish corrections in your body memory patterns, and you won't need to pay such close attention to placement as time passes.

Now, turn back to the "Anatomy of the Foot" on page 39, and find the abductor hallicus tendon and its muscle. Note how it attaches directly to the side of the big toe. This is where the bunion protrudes. Contracting this muscle draws the big toe outward. Strengthening this muscle can assist your big toe in not curving inward. **NEVER** wear pointed shoes no matter how stylish. Finally, give your feet a nice massage and warm bath as often as you can, and rub out any tension around your toes and insteps.

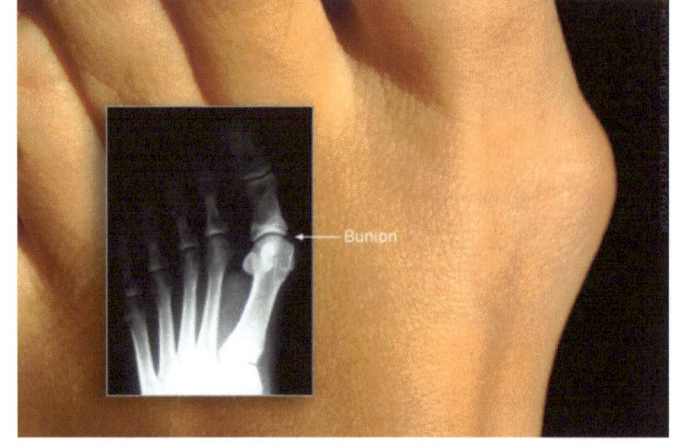

*F.Y.I. Pointe work in properly fitting shoes won't cause bunions.*

# EXERCISES for the Big Toe

**Purpose:** To strengthen big toe muscles and help in dealing with bunions.

"Most foot pain is entirely preventable and reversible through a thoughtfully-designed exercise routine. Fallen arches, inflamed fascia, and over-tight foot muscles are all created through movement habits and can quickly improve when those habits are corrected."

BIOMECHANIST KATY BOWMAN

## Technique

**BIG TOE SPREAD W/BAND**
Maintain your tripod stand throughout. After mastering, do toe spread without band.

**TOE SPREADING**
Relax the ankle and don't allow the tendons on top of the foot to tense up. This exercise strengthens the abductor hallicus as well as others.

**BIG TOE EXERCISE**
Resist both on the lift and the return on this exercise.

### Big Toe Spread w/Band
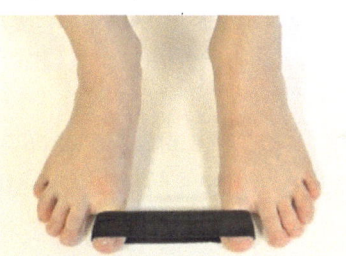
Place your big toes between a thick piece of elastic or rubber band, pull apart until taunt. Hold 20 counts. Repeat often daily.

### Big Toe Spread w/Eyelashes
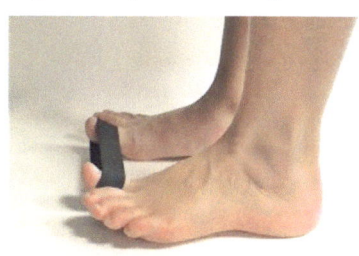
Keeping the big toes spread apart, do the "Eyelashes" exercise.

### Toe Spread
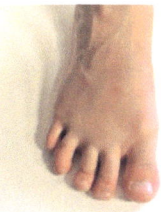
Spread your toes apart as far as possible. Use your fingers to open your big toe outward, if needed.

### Doming
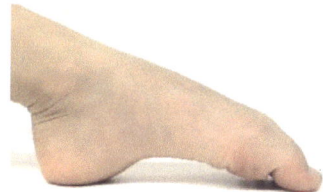
Do doming often using spacers or your fingers to keep the big toe from pulling inward.

**Big Toe Exercise** - strengthens the Flexor Hallucis Brevis which not only moves the big toe but supports the arch.

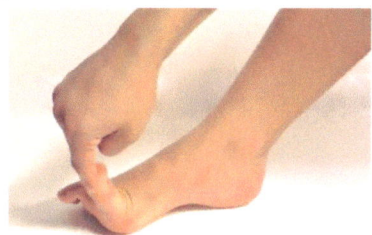
*Hold big toe up with fingers.*

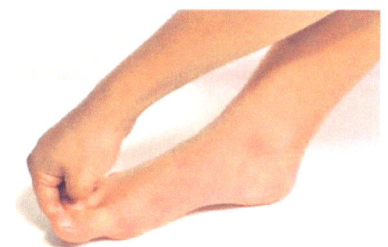
*Resist toe pulling fingers down.*

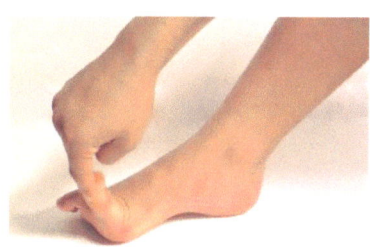
*Resist pulling toe up. Do 10x.*

# WEAK FEET AND Rolling Ankles

Rolling ankles and weak feet are perhaps the most damaging fault a dancer can have. This weakness not only affects your feet, ankles and knees, but your entire body. It hampers your ability to balance and leap and exposes you to serious injury.

The action of rolling inward flattens the plantar fascia (see pages 61 & 62) beneath your foot causing it to pull taunt. This leaves it vulnerable to small tears as the fascia is called on to stretch beyond its limits —as in landing a jump. These tears can cause heel pain called plantar fasciitis and may also lead to heel spurs. Not only that, but rolling in with your ankles stretches the ligaments on the inside of your foot and ankle weakening this area even more.

I can't say enough about the necessity for correcting flat or pronating feet! If you have this problem, do lots of foot and ankle strengthening exercises particularly the Doming and Elevé Series as well as elevés on a step. Exercise alone, however, will not correct this fault. You must train yourself to continually think about keeping your weight over your balancing points making sure that your ankles are pulled up throughout each class and your knees stay over your toes. Do not allow yourself to roll.

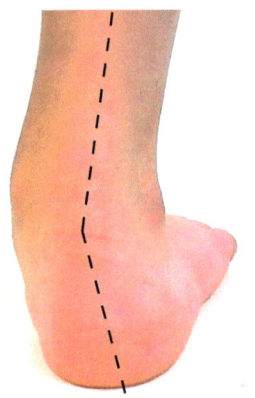 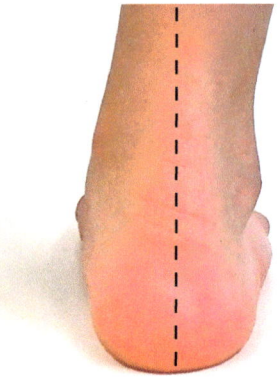

*Rolling Ankle - Pronated*          *Correctly Held Ankle in Tripod Strand*

# **ANKLE** Strengthening

**Purpose:** Strengthening the outer and inner muscles which control the ankle.

## Strengthening the Ankles

**The Flair:** Seated with a theraband wrapped around your foot and heel and secured to a stationary object on the inside of your foot. Flair your foot slowly outward and hold 5 counts. Slowly return your foot to center. Do 10x.

**The Sickle:** Same as above with the theraband on the outside.

**The Elevé:** Stand on two feet in parallel with a theraband wrapped around one ankle and heel. Step away from the stationary area so the theraband is taunt. Slowly elevé straight up, keeping your foot and ankle balanced correctly between the big and 2nd toes. Hold 5 counts. Turn and repeat on the other foot.

**Outward/Inward Sweeps Seated or Standing:** Can be done with a towel on the floor.

**Heel Pivots:** Pivoting your heel on the floor, sweep only your foot outward - not your knee and lower leg. Return to center. Outward sweeps strengthen the muscles of the outer ankle, and inward sweeps strengthen - you guessed it - the inner muscles. Do 10x.

**Isometric Wall Press Seated or Standing:** Beside an immovable flat surface (like a wall), press your foot outward or inward against that surface. Hold 5 counts and repeat.

### *Technique*

1. Keep toes stretched long and relaxed throughout these exercises.

2. Use only your ankle to flair or sickle. Do not use your leg by turning out or in.

3. When you've finished, do full ankle rotations to release of muscle tension.

4. Train yourself to immediately correct any rolling that happens in your ankles.

**Elevés on a step are great for foot, ankle, and lower leg strength.**

# FOOT AND ANKLE MASSAGE

## TAKING CARE OF YOUR FEET WITH MASSAGE

Our feet are the most overworked part of our body and usually quite neglected. Tired, hard working feet deserve to be well cared for. Begin with warming them up with a bath, rubdown or wrap them in a warm, moist towel. Got a golf ball? Well, after they are worn, put one under your foot and roll it around on the floor. Ahhhh . . . *Linger a while in any sore areas you come across.* Dancers on pointe or taking several classes a week need to make a habit of this wonderful tool for releasing stored tension.

## MASSAGING YOUR TOES

- Holding one toe at a time between your thumb and index finger, rub your thumb along the sides, top and bottom of each toe.
- Holding as above, squeeze the top and pull each toe.
- Holding as above with the thumb on top pull your finger out from the base of each toe.
- Take the end of each toe, wiggle it gently up and down, back and forth, twist and circle.
- Sandwich your toes between your hands and hold flat for a few minutes.

## MORE MASSAGES

### PLANTAR FASCIA MASSAGE

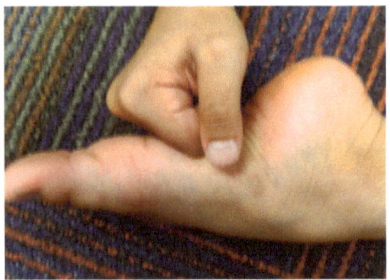

*Starting at the ball of the foot, slide knuckles up your sole. You can also pull the toes back with the other hand while you do this.*

### BETWEEN THE FOOT BONES

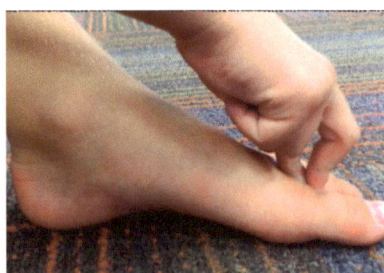

*Using the same hand as foot, place 2nd finger on top of 1st and press between big toe and 2nd toe.*

### INSIDE OF THE ACHILLES

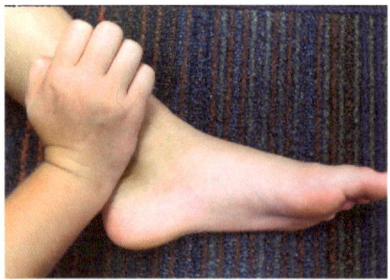

*On the inside of the foot, use the heel of the hand (little finger side) to rub from inside the heel beside the tendon pulling upward to the calf.*

# FOOT AND ANKLE CARE

## FOOT CARE PRODUCTS

There are many products designed for the care of your feet from gel pads to toe braces, from arch sleeves to orthotics. There are even footcare kits just for dancers, which range from skin care lotions, scrubs and soaks to mole skin, adhesives and antiseptic pads (to ward off infection). You can also make up your own kit.

- **Blister care -** Patches, plasters, mole skin, adhesive pads, silicone gel sheets, compressed wool felt, toe tape, sprays, toe caps
- **Bunions -** Bunion guards, splints, slings, gel toe spacers or separators
- **Insoles and Orthotics -** Gel, moldable, semi-flexible and non-flexible inserts
- **Pads -** for the ball, heel or instep
- **Braces and Bands -** for arch and ankle support
- **Pointe shoe padding -** gels, foam, silicone and lambs wool toe pads, lambs wool heel pads

Dancers need healthy feet so give them special care on a weekly basis so poor care won't lead to foot problems.

- Keep your feet clean, dry, and moisturized.
- Trim toe nails not too short, straight across, and not in at the edges - this can lead to ingrown toe nails.
- Cover any blisters with a bandaid or tape.
- Be sure your shoes fit properly.
- Stretch and massage your feet regularly, to ensure your feet remain flexible and released from tension.

# ASSESSMENTS #5 - #8

### #5 and #6 - Seated Pointe Range

| | |
|---|---|
| **Purpose** | To determine if each foot is sufficiently arched for pointe work. |
| **Determining your pointe range:** | Sit on the floor with one leg extended forward and your foot pointed until parallel to the floor. Under extended feet will not allow a dancer to rise fully onto the platform of her pointe shoes without bending her knees. Being placed on pointe with an inadequate pointe range is extremely frustrating, awkward, and dangerous. |
| **Correction:** | Your seated pointe range can be stretched with persistent daily stretching, particularly if you are still young. |

### #7 and #8 - Elevé Pointe Range

| | |
|---|---|
| **Purpose:** | To determine if each foot has sufficient strength and big toe flexibility to elevé to full demi-pointe. This is measured by forming a line perpendicular to the floor from metatarsal bone to ankle bone. |
| **Inadequate Strength:** | If you have passed tests 3 and 4 but can't pass these two tests, it means one of two things:<br>1. Your feet have the flexibility but not the strength you need to rise to a full pointe.<br>2. You have a stiff big toe which keeps you from rising fully. |
| **Strengthening or stretching:** | Create a daily foot exercises program to fit your needs and diligently repeat it 3 to 4 times per day - this will help you achieve your goal. |

# Assessments #5 - #8

| ASSESSMENTS | REQUIREMENTS TO PASS |
|---|---|
| **#5 and #6 - Seated Pointe Range** | When a straight edge is placed between the ankle and big toe metatarsal bone, it must lie at least parallel with the floor. Toes must remain straight and not curl under when pointing.<br>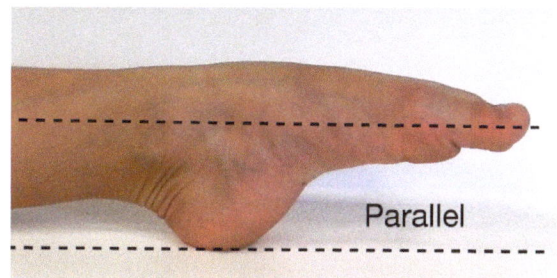 |
| **#7 and #8 - Elevé Pointe Range** | Elevé in parallel on one straight leg and hold the wall or barre. A line between your big toe's metatarsal bone and the center of your ankle bone must reach a minimum of 90° with the floor in order to pass.<br>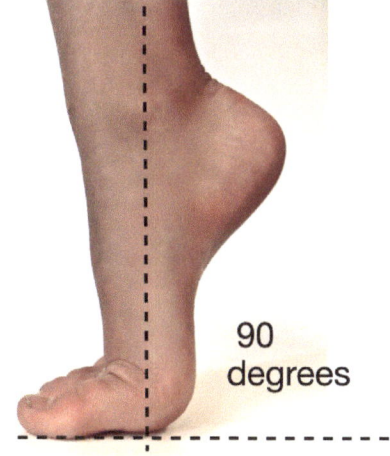 |

# INJURIES TO THE FOOT AND ANKLE

Dancers can experience injury when suddenly rolling, sickling, twisting, jerking or jamming their foot or ankle. This is likely to happen when landing a poorly-placed jump, in a quick direction change, or with an unexpected trip or fall.

Most minor injuries heal on their own with home treatment involving icing, rest, and taping or wrapping for support. A severe injury, however, needs to be seen by a doctor.

**The best protection a dancer has for preventing injury is in her training.**

Developing strength within the small muscles within your feet creates a sound foundation for pointe work and is a necessity for injury prevention.

| THE BASICS | COMMON INJURIES OF THE FOOT/ANKLE |
|---|---|
| | **SUDDEN FORCE INJURIES** |
| A. Land all jumps with toe, ball, heel, plié. | 1. Sprains: Injuries to the ligaments of a joint, occur when ligaments are overstretched. Ankle ligaments are the most common injuries. |
| B. Keep knees over the toes in all plié movements. | 2. Strain: Pulled muscles or tendons from overstretching causes small tears in these fibers. A strain is to a muscle as a sprain is to a ligament. |
| | **OVERUSE INJURIES** *(Too much stress on a joint or tissue.)* |
| C. Warm up the feet and ankles well before jumping. | 3. Bursitis: Inflammation of the bursa (small fluid-filled pads), causing swelling and tenderness in the heel. Pain is usually worse when wearing shoes and during activity but improves with rest. |
| D. Do not overly push yourself when fatigued. | 4. Tendinitis: Inflammation of a tendon. For dancers, the Achilles or Patellar tendon (Jumper's knee). |
| E. Maintain your concentration while dancing. | 5. Plantar Fasciitis: Inflammation of the plantar fascia. (See next page.) |
| | 6. Stress Fracture: A hairline crack in a bone. |
| | 7. Metatarsalgia: Pain in ball of the foot. |

# PAIN IN YOUR FEET

"The human foot is a masterpiece of engineering and a work of art," said Leonardo da Vinci. Our feet allow us to move in fantastic ways. We can, however, experience a lot of pain when things go wrong.

Your feet are designed with 3 dynamic arches. Dynamic, meaning they give and flex as we move rather than remaining fixed. There's a complex group of muscles and fascia supporting these arches, and they work together to power each movement.

## PLANTAR FASCIA

The plantar fascia is an extraordinary structure which runs along the bottom of your foot from heel to toes and arch to arch. It's important for propelling you when walking, running, jumping, or leaping. It supports the arch and is designed to absorb the high stresses and strains placed upon your feet daily. The plantar fascia does not stretch, and isn't supposed to, for it provides structural tension which is needed to support your body.

The plantar fascia is designed to cope with strain in an on/off way rather than remain under a constant load. Weakness in muscles which support your foot (as with flat feet) places a constant strain on the plantar fascia, and it can start to hurt at the heel. This is called Plantar Fasciitis.

> *NOTE: With arched feet, the fascia is floppy and not pulling at the heel. When the arch is flattened, as is the case with flat feet, the plantar fascia is stretched taunt when standing and pulls on its insertion point at the heel bone. This constant stress can create small tears in the fascia and can produce heel spurs.*

Strain can result from jarred landings, strength imbalances between feet, rolling, and gripping the floor with the big toes. Even when dancing on a sprung floor, dancers must land jumps using proper toe, ball, heel, plié for the best possible shock absorption. An overladed and overstretched plantar fascia can develop small tears causing inflammation and heel pain. This is plantar fasciitis.

## Points for Avoiding or Healing Plantar Fasciitis

- Prevent your ankles from rolling throughout the day as well as in your dance classes.
- Arch supports can be worn in street shoes for a while until you build up sufficient foot and ankle strength.
- Stretch through the back of your body, especially the lower legs. Do lots of calf stretches.
- While healing, avoid re-straining an injured plantar fascia with rest and gentle support to reduce the load it carries.
- Avoid massage and stretches for the bottom of your foot for this will probably worsen the problem.
- Develop stronger muscular support for the arches of your foot by doing lots of foot strengthening exercises.

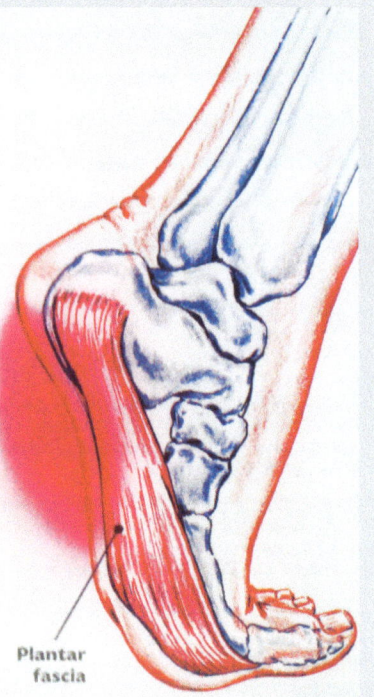

Plantar fascia

## Flexibility Through the Back

Our plantar fascia is directly connected to the fascia running along the full back of our body. Described as the "Superficial Back Line" tension anywhere within the back can cause pulling and tension down into the sole of your foot. Therefore, it's very important in dealing with plantar fascia issues, to stretch out through the entire back line of your body.

## Supporting the Plantar Fascia

Providing support to the plantar fascia with a shoe insert is essential to allow inflammation to ease while you build strength in your feet and ankles to control your feet yourself. There are all kinds of inserts available. Try them in your school and running shoes and taping for dance classes. The best taping technique creates a cross woven web over the sole of the foot which mimics the plantar fascia. Another technique I've heard about actually uses a theraband taped to the sole of the foot mimicking the plantar fascia.

# Ingrown Toenails

An ingrown toenail occurs when the edge of a toenail grows down and into the skin rather than over it. Those with curved thick nails are more at risk.

Ingrown toenails are usually caused from cutting your nails too short or back on the sides and not straight across. You can even develop an ingrown nail after stubbing or jamming your toe.

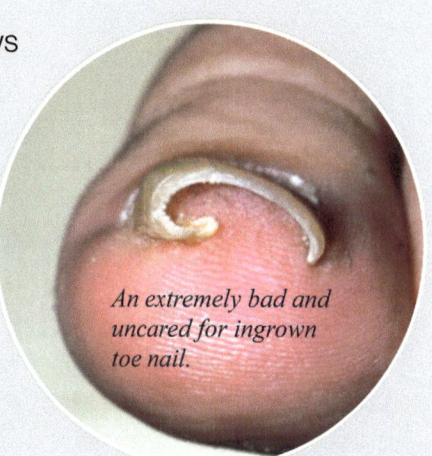

*An extremely bad and uncared for ingrown toe nail.*

Ingrown toenails may become irritated and create pain, redness, and swelling. They may, if they become infected, need the care of a doctor.

Home remedies from the Mayo Clinic: Soak feet for 20 minutes 3x/day in warm water to reduce swelling and tenderness. Follow by placing cotton or dental floss under the ingrown side of the nail after soaking. (This will help the nail to eventually grow out above the skin.) Use a topical antibiotic and bandage. Wear open-toed shoes or sandals. If the pain becomes severe or spreads, see your doctor to relieve the discomfort and avoid complications.

People who have conditions that cause poor circulation in the feet such as diabetes are at greater risk of developing complications from ingrown nails.

Self-care can be successful if caught early, but remember the best treatment is prevention. Take good care of your feet and nails.

## Appearance of Toe

- Skin will appear to grow over the nail.
- Nail appears to grow under skin.
- Skin swollen, red, firm, and or tender to the touch.

## Treatment

- Soak in warm water 3 or 4 times a day.
- Easily massage area of concern.
- Place a small amount of cotton w/ antiseptic under nail.

## Causes

- Cutting the edges of your nail curved instead of straight.
- Cutting the nail too short.
- Poorly-fitting shoes.
- After an injury.

## Pain in The Ball Of The Foot

1. If the ball of your foot has tenderness over the whole area, it may be that you are landing too heavily on the ball of your foot and are not controlling your instep when landing.

2. En Pointe - If the pain is under the ball of the second toe, check to see if your second toe is longer than your big toe. In this case you might create a "custom-made (from regular strapping tape) toe thong with supports to offload the tip of the second metatarsal." said Lisa Howell "This is a GREAT tip and will also help students to balance more on demi-pointe."

3. Sesamoiditis - There are two small bones at the base of the big toe, and irritation of the tissues around these sesamoid bones can cause pain. The FHL (flexor hallucis longus) tendon is located between them and can become irritated, especially with a lot of demi-pointe work. The cause can actually be due to stiffness in the joint on the big toe, which would result in an increased load on its metatarsal when walking and dancing.

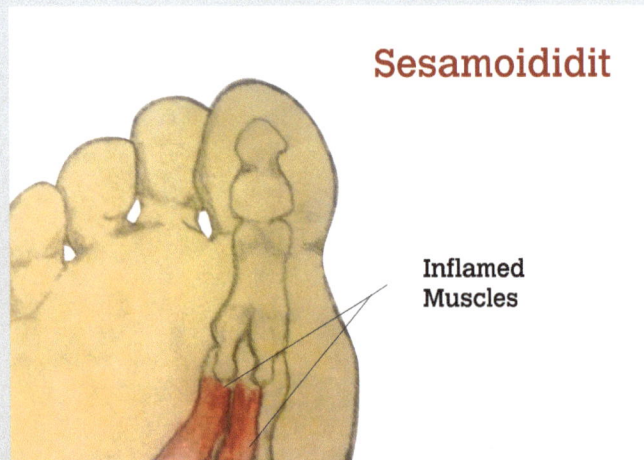

### Sesamoididit

Inflamed Muscles

## TURNED ANKLE

Sprains are sudden, acute injuries that can significantly affect a dancer's ability to perform and participate in class.

Should an ankle sprain occur:

1. Icing is most effective immediately following the injury and can be applied several times a day for 15 to 20 minutes directly on the injury. Move the ice frequently and don't allow it to sit too long in one spot as frostbite can occur.

2. Allow 45 minutes between ice applications.

3. Elevate the leg - this also helps with swelling.

4. Rest off that foot for a few days.

5. Protect the sprained ankle: **DON'T WALK ON A SPRAINED ANKLE.**

A dancer is exposed to ankle sprains when landing jumps, leaps, or in turning. This is especially true if a dancer is overly tired, distracted, or loses concentration in technique or alignment.

Dancers with weak ankles or who have reoccurring ankle sprains are especially at risk.

# ACHILLES TENDINOPATHY OR A RUPTURE

There are two main reasons for Achilles pain. Tendinopathy, which is either tendinitis (inflammation of the achilles), or tendinosis (tiny tears in the tendon). Pain in your achilles, which often won't even allow your heels to lower when standing yet does improve as you walk around, is most likely the beginning stages of achilles tendinopathy. If this pain persists and is not treated, it can result in a ruptured tendon, the second reason for achilles pain. A rupture or tear in your achilles generally happens from a sudden forceful motion that places a lot of stress on your calf such as pushing off or landing wrong during jumps. There are other conditions causing pain behind the ankle so be sure to see your doctor for a correct diagnosis.

The goal of treatment is to reduce your pain and strengthen your tendon. It must cover every factor which has contributed to this problem including: 1. an eccentric loading exercise program 2. core and pelvic stability work 3. foot control and 4. temporarily, a restricted activity schedule. Make sure your therapist helps you address all these contributing factors. Tending to the pain early can help you avoid these problems.

## *Prevention is always better than a cure!*

- Create strong muscles under your foot.
- Correct rolling ankles (in or out).
- Always plié with your knees over your toes.
- Do elevés on a stair and single leg pliés in parallel.
- Do core stability exercises.
- Always do calf stretches after lots of jumps or elevé work.

# Chapter 3

## ASSESSMENTS 9 - 14

## *Knees and Legs*

The gorgeous line of a ballerina's legs causes us to marvel at their perfection. They allow her to dance with fluid, effortlessness grace. It's not so much her extension that gains our attention, but her placement, line, flow, and control that puts us in awe.

# SUMMARY
## *Chapter 3*
# KNEES AND LEGS

The incredible legs of a dancer are gained through stretching, strengthening, and fantastic technique.

## ABOUT YOUR LOWER LEG MUSCLES:

These muscles work with your foot for supporting, balancing and propelling your body. A common overuse injury in the front of the lower leg is shin splints. Weak foot muscles can contribute to this condition. Also common - tightness in the calf - needs calf stretches, especially after alegro work.

## ABOUT YOUR KNEE:

Our knees are the largest, most complex joints in our body. They are created by 4 ligaments attaching the femur of our upper leg to the tibia and fibula of our lower leg as well as the ligament and tendon in front holding our patella. Muscles attach in the upper and lower leg to bend and extend our knees.

## THE OFTEN NEGLECTED DEMI-PLIÉ:

Learn to use your demi-plié deeply, always opening knees well over the toes. Apply it to soften and fill your adage movements, create fluid transitions between steps and absorb the shock of alegro landings as well as strongly propelling you into the air.

## ABOUT YOUR UPPER LEG MUSCLES:

The muscles of the upper leg are important for walking, running, propelling, splits, grand battements, développé, and much, much more. Strong, flexible upper leg muscles are the goal of all dancers.

## MANAGING YOUR LEGS:

Hyperextended legs must be managed so as not to cause injury and pain. Learning to hold the knees straight while bearing weight and not allowing them to slip back is a constant task, but can be mastered. Hypoextended legs can be somewhat corrected through gentle stretching and strengthening. Bowed and knocked legs can also be corrected by correctly holding them stretched in ballet class.

# MUSCLES OF THE LOWER LEG

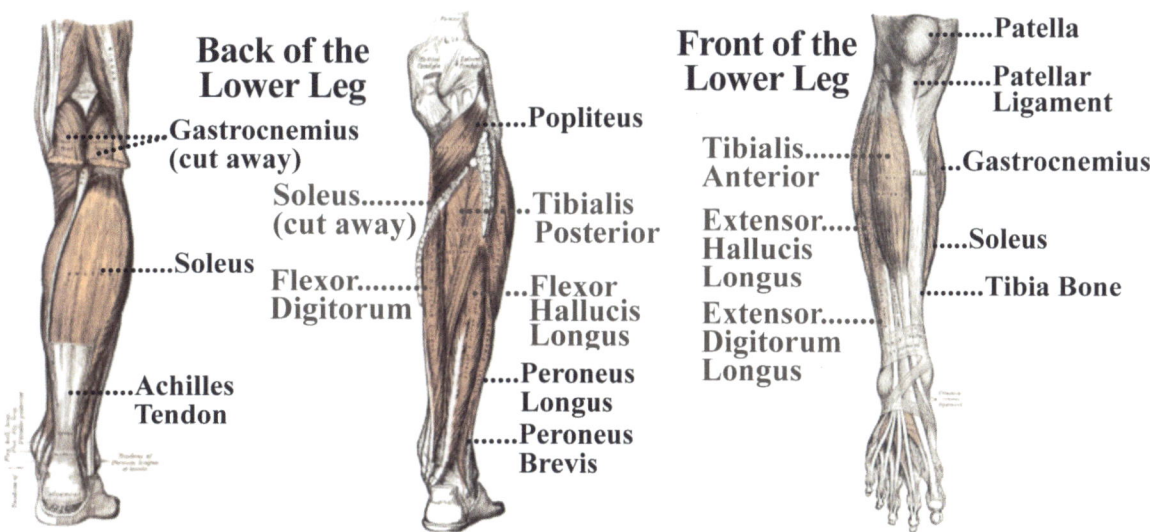

## BACK OF THE LOWER LEG

**Gastrocnemius** is a very powerful, bulging two-headed calf muscle used for pointing and pushing when we're walking, running, or jumping.

**Soleus** is a wider, flatter muscle which lies beneath the gastrocnemius. It's used constantly when standing and keeping us upright. These two muscles merge into the achilles tendon. Tightness in the calf can be a possible reason for pain in the achilles.

**Flexor Hallucis Longus** is the largest and strongest of the deep lower leg muscles. It flexes the big toe and helps somewhat in pointing.

**Tibialis Posterior** is located deep in back of the lower leg. It supports our foot's main arch, and both points and sickles the foot.

**Peroneus Longus** goes from the outer knee, downward and across the bottom of the foot to where the big toe bones begins. It flairs and points the foot.

**Peroneus Brevis,** located under the peroneus longus, flexes and flairs the foot and supports the longitudinal arch.

## FRONT OF THE LOWER LEG

**Tibialis Anterior** is located on the outside of the tibia bone and if overused, can result in shin splints. It flexes and sickles the foot and is strongly involved when balancing as it supports the medial arch (our main arch).

**Extensor Digitorum Longus** lifts the little toes upward (on page 41).

**Extensor Hallucis Longus** is a thin muscle, located by the extensor digitorum longus which lifts the big toe upward.

# CALF STRETCHING Series

**Purpose:** To establish equal plié depth to 2 1/2" for shorter girls and 4 1/2" for taller girls.

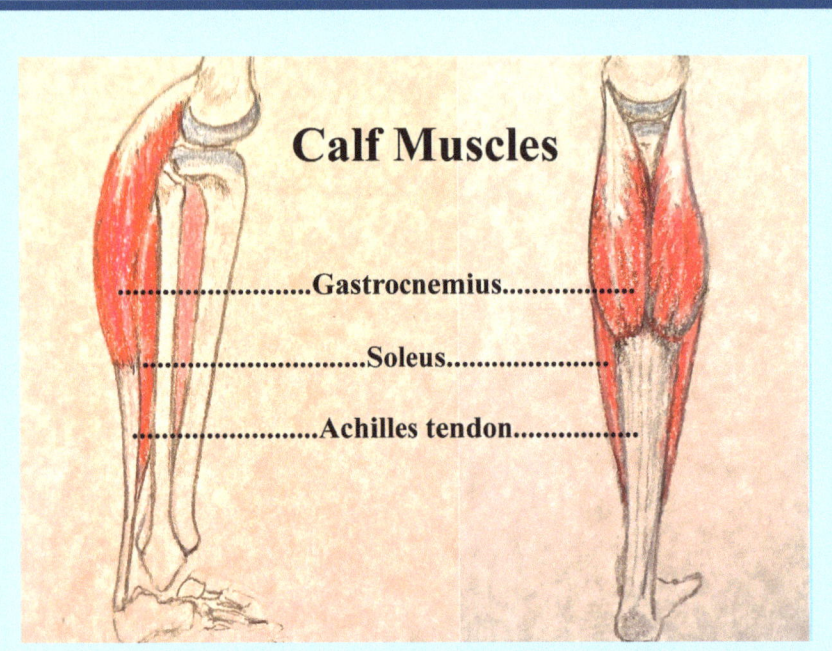

GASTROCNEMIUS: The largest muscle of the calf. The main muscle when walking or running.

SOLEUS: A wider, flatter muscle which lies beneath the gastrocnemius. It is used constantly when standing keeping us upright.

*These two muscles attach to the achilles tendon. (A tight calf is a possible reason for pain in the achilles.)*

## Technique

1. **Gastrocnemius Stretch:** In lunge with heels directly behind the toes. Keep your hips square and hold for 10 counts. Rest 3 counts and repeat. Change legs. Repeat.

2. **Soleus Stretch:** As above with weight shifted onto the back leg in plié. Shorten your stance. Keep your hips square and hold 10 counts. Rest 3 counts and Repeat. Change legs. Repeat.

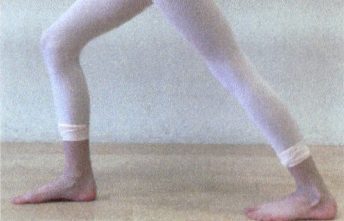

*Gastrocnemius Stretch: Lunge forward w/heels on floor directly behind toes.*

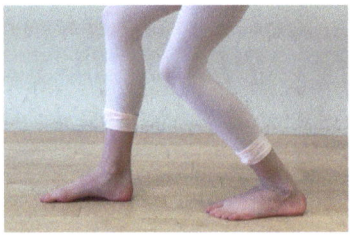

*Soleus Stretch: In shorter stance, plié on back leg as far as possible.*

*1 and 2 Combination Stretch: Keep back straight.*

# CALF STRENGTHENING Series

**Purpose:** To build strength in your calfs, ankles and feet necessary for jumps and rising to full height in elevé.

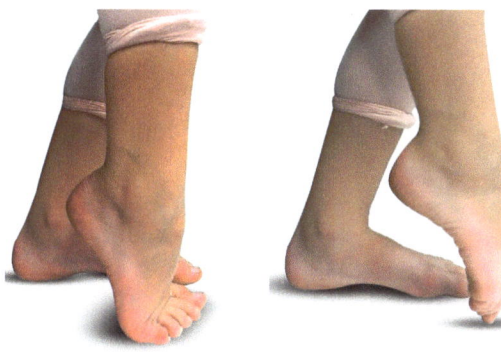

### Seated elevés as shown before
Seated with feet flat on floor. Rest your arms on one leg and press that heel up 5 counts (concentric phase) then lower 5 counts (eccentric phase). Do 10 on each leg 2 sets every other day. Advanced version.

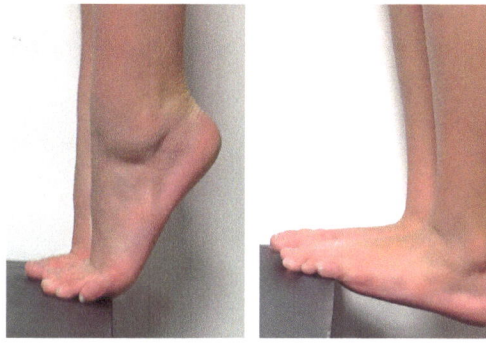

### Double or Single Leg elevés on a Step

Rise to your highest in 5 counts (Concentric Phase). Lower 5 counts (eccentric phase).

Do 15x - 2 sets every other day.

Variations: 1. Do in parallel then turnout
2. Do in turnout with plié
3. Do with straight leg bending forward from hip.

## Why Can't I Reach My Full Demi-Pointe Height?

The other side of not being able to stretch your foot to a full pointe when seated is not being able to rise to a full demi-pointe when standing. Strengthening exercises for the feet and calf must be done daily. In class, diligently rise to your highest demi-pointe each time you elevé. Stretch the backs of your toes or front of your ankles if you have tightness in these areas.

NOTE: Foot strengthening exercises are covered in the Foot and Ankle chapter as well as Toe Stretches.

## Technique

**Seated elevés:**

When pressing up to the ball of your foot, hold your weight between the big and 2nd toe. Keep your heel behind your toes.

**Elevés On A Step:**

Do this exercise slowly, and don't rush. As above, don't roll out or in as you rise. Pull up tall through your knees.

# OUR AMAZING KNEES!

## ALTHOUGH LOOKING SIMPLE, OUR KNEES ARE QUITE COMPLEX AND WITHOUT CARE, CAN BE INJURED.

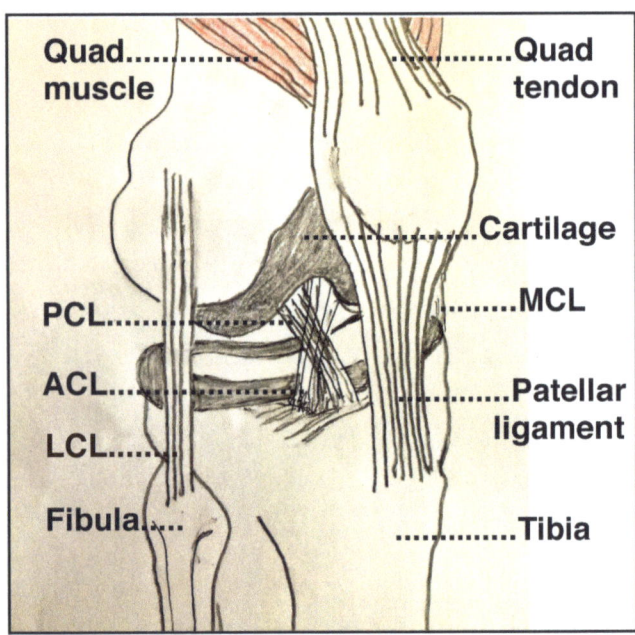

### THE MAKEUP OF OUR KNEES!

*Four bones:* the femur (upper leg bone), the tibia (large lower leg bone), the fibula (small lower leg bone) and the patella (knee cap).

*Ligaments:* Four ligaments stabilize and hold our knee together - the LCL AND MCL on the sides and the PCL and ACL in the center.

*Meniscus:* The cartilage which lines the bones allowing movement to slide freely.

*Bursa:* Small fluid filled sacs helping the knee to move smoothly.

Taking good care of your knees before there's a problem is extremely important for dancers. The primary function of the knee is to flex and extend. It can also slightly rotate and tilt - probably the main reason for knee injuries.

Ligament and meniscus tears are unfortunately common. So, when dancing make sure you take care of your knees by doing the following:

- Any time you plié, make sure your knees are always over your toe, especially when on one leg. Many dancers allow their knee to roll inward at this time.

- Land all jumps with toe, ball, heel, plié.

- Never turnout from your knees. I've seen too many dancers plié placing their feet in 1st or 5th in a 180° degree turnout, then straighten their knees twisting them with the turnout their hips can't achieve.

# MASTERING Plié

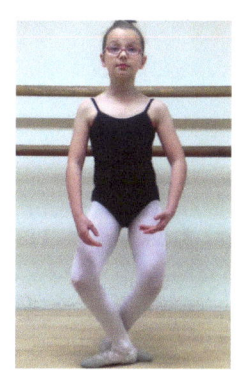

Plié (to bend) is a primary building block of ballet and definitely under used both in class and performances. Demi-plié is often called a dancer's best friend as it, along with your feet and ankles, propels you into the air and absorbs the shock of landing. It also releases calf tension, and contributes greatly to a dancer's elegant fluidity.

## COMPONENTS OF A CORRECTLY EXECUTED DEMI PLIÉ

1. **Master core control:** As in tendu, your demi-plié begins by engaging the core.

2. **Whether standing on one or two legs, be continually aware of your turnout muscles, and building their endurance:** The piriformis muscles, illiopoas, adductors, and sartorius all need to be engaged when turing out.

3. **Control the position of your knees:** Holding your knees over your toes in all plié movements is of utmost importance to knee safety. The bad habit of continually allowing them to roll inward stretches the ligaments on the inside of the knee, and leaves a dancer open to painful injuries.

4. **A correctly executed demi-plié:** Before you even begin your plié, stretch upward and away from your hips and engage your core and turnout muscles, keeping your feet firmly held in their tripod stand. Slowly and deeply bend opening the knees over your toes without allowing your heels to lift. Feel the calves stretch. Smoothly return making sure your knees are held opened and not allowed to roll inward. Hold your hips, back and shoulders in neutral throughout your plié.

5. **Grand Plié:** The first 1/4 of your grand plié is a demi-plié. As you lower further, don't lift your heels but rather allow them to leave the floor as little as possible. The depth is established just before you lose control or before allowing your calves to touch your thighs - <u>never sit at the bottom of your grand plié</u>. Immediately begin pressing your heels down and return to demi-plié and the final 1/4.

**CHECK LIST:** *Back, hips, and shoulders remain erect throughout the entire plié. Knees don't roll inward, especially as your grand plié begins rising. Heels press down as soon as possible Grand pliés are smooth, continuous and don't sit at the bottom. Arm and head movements are complementary and equally smooth.*

# MUSCLES of the Inner Thigh

## YOUR LINK TO BALANCE AND TURNOUT

"The inner thigh has more to do with the function of your leg and your ability to move in any direction whether it is stable (riding a bike) or not (running)."
YOUTH TO THE CORE

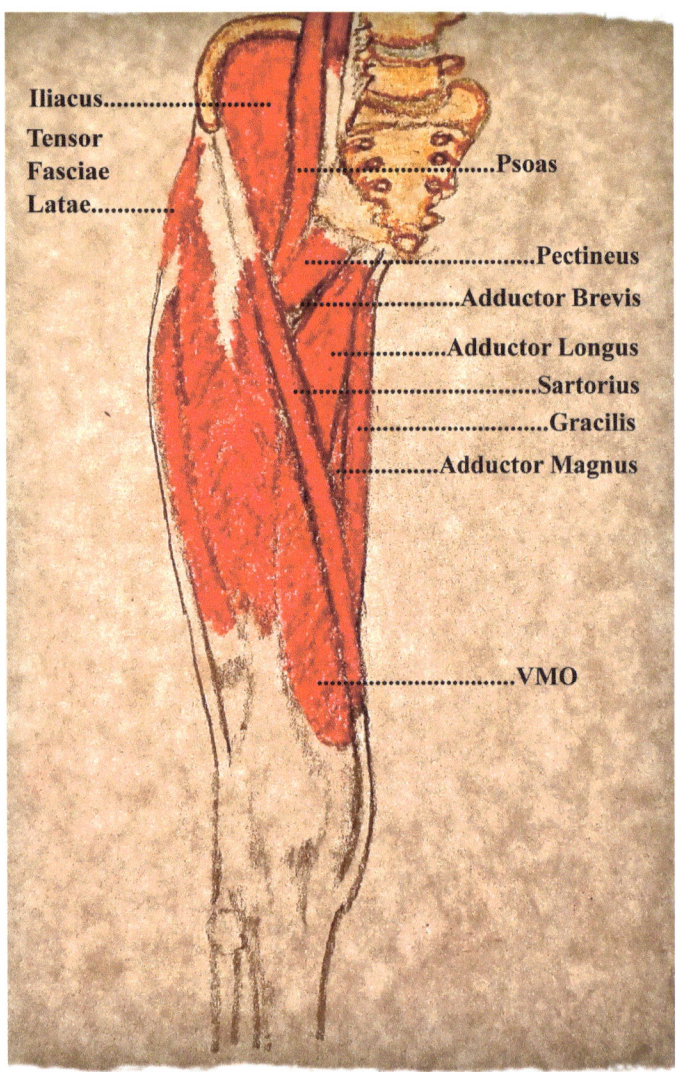

### ADDUCTORS

They work together to pull the thigh toward center as well as help lift the leg in turnout.

**Pectineus:** a flat muscle that attaches in the front of the pelvis and runs downward and back to the femur. It is primarily responsible for lifting the leg. It also helps pull the leg in and rotate it inward.

**Adductor Brevis:** a smaller superficial muscle which mainly pulls the leg inward as well as lifting it up.

**Adductor Longus**: a longer wider superficial muscle which main action is to move the thigh inwards and outwardly rotate it.

**Adductor Magnus:** a large triangular muscle which lies beneath the adductors brevis and longus and attaches to most of the femur's length. It is powerful for pulling the leg inward. When strengthened sufficiently, it can lift the body up from the splits. It also aids in turnout as well.

**Gracilis:** the most superficial adductor muscle located on the inside of the thigh. It can be overextended when stretching into the splits.

NOTE: The sartorius is not technically an adductor - it rotates the leg outward as in turnout. All muscles discussed attach to the pelvis and are involved with all movements of the pelvis. This makes them vulnerable to pulls and strains. Be cautious, and stretch only after warming up and work them slowly.

# THE INNER THIGH Series

**Purpose:** To train the inner thigh correctly. Because these muscles are weak compared to the tissue and muscles around them, stretch and strengthen them gently. Avoid stretching or fatiguing them completely as they can be injured more easily.

## Technique

### Strengthening

1. Engage your core first.
2. Hold spine in neutral, not allowing the waist to lower to the floor.
3. Hold hips stacked for duration of exercise.
4. Inhale while lifting. Exhale while lowering and don't strain.

### Stretching

1. Stop if there is any pain in knee or inner groin.
2. Don't do stretch if you feel pressure in the hip socket.

## Strengthening the Inner Thigh

### Beginning

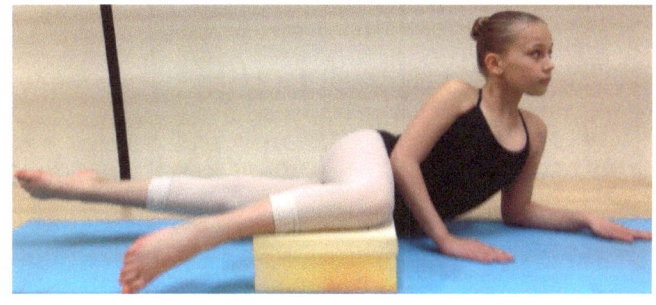

Slowly lift straight leg off the floor about 6 inches. Hold for 5 sec. Slowly lower to floor. Do 10x.

### Advanced

Repeat 1st exercise holding 30 sec. Lift again and bend knee toward other knee then straighten 10x. Repeat 1st exercise 10x.

Adjust the repetitions and hold time to your own strength.

## Stretching the Inner Thigh

### Short Inner Thigh Stretch        Long Inner Thigh Stretch

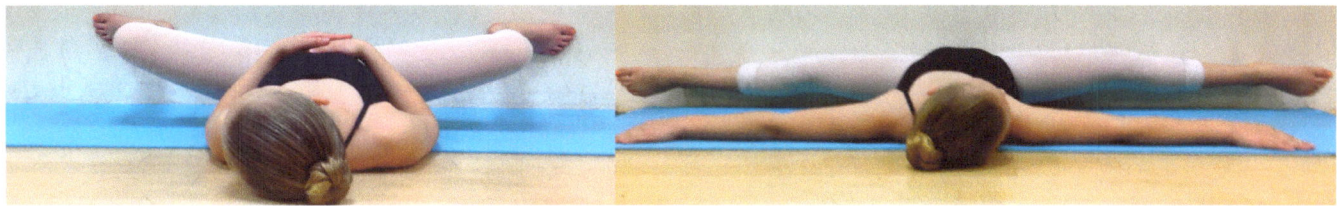

With feet 6 inches above the floor on a wall and knees bent in line with hips, lower knees as far as possible. Hold for 30 sec. Move knees up and down a little between holds, working the muscles in the hip. Do 2x. Repeat.

Lay with bottom against wall with legs up the wall. Lower sideways and hold. Moving your legs from time to time allows for more stretch. Do 3x then move the feet inward 90° like short inner thigh stretch and out again. Do 5x.

# MUSCLES in the Back of the Thigh

## POWERFUL MUSCLES WHICH MOVE YOU FORWARD

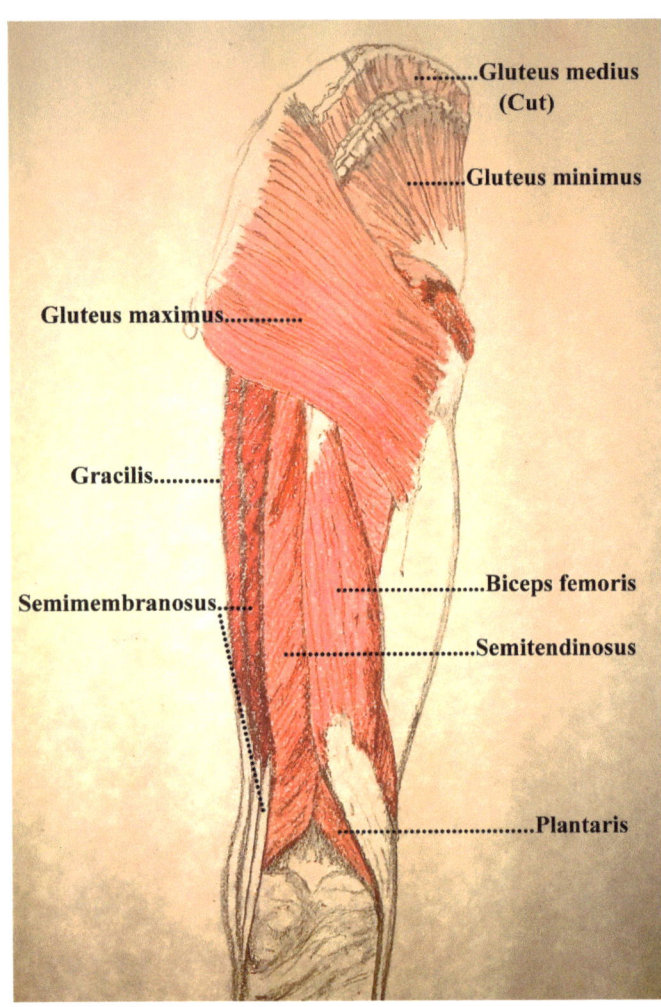

*In our modern society hamstring stiffness is quite common due to the fact that most people sit on chairs for long periods of time with much less siting on the ground and bending over as our ancestors did. In ballet it is very important to have flexible hamstrings for your extension.*

### GLUTEALS

**Gluteus maximus** - lifts the leg derrière, supports the pelvis and trunk when standing on one leg, and launches us forward and upward.

**Gluteus medius and minimus** - pull the leg out to the side; they also hold the hips stable when on one leg, and in retiré they help turnout the thigh.

### HAMSTRINGS

A group of three, mainly fast twitch, muscles located in the back of the thigh. They act upon the knee and hip joints extending the hip in arabesque derrière and flexing the knee in attitude. The biceps femoris is the most often injured followed by the semitendinosis. They aren't very active when walking or standing, but are extremely active when running, jumping or climbing.

**Biceps femoris** - the outermost of the hamstrings.

**Semitendinosus** - the center hamstring having an extremely long tendon.

**Semimembranosus** - the innermost of the hamstrings and is chronically tight. It can often contribute to lower back pain because of this tightness.

# THE HAMSTRING Series

**Purpose:** Usually it's not weak but tight hamstrings which are the case. For dancers, tight hamstrings are unthinkable. If this is your concern, be consistent and diligently complete a daily program of these stretching exercises.

## Strengthening the Back of the Thigh

**Beginning:** Stand in parallel 2nd with both feet standing on a theraband and each hand holding an end to your shoulders. Bend forward in plié, with a flat back. Straighten back and legs. Do 10x.

**Advanced:** Stand on theraband as above. Keep your legs straight and bend forward from the hips. Holding the ends of the band, fold hands behind neck. Keeping legs straight, pull torso up to an erect position with back straight. Do 10x.

## Stretching the Back of the Thigh

**The Classic:** Seated with legs front. Reach forward to touch toes. Hold 10 counts. Do 5x.

**One Leg Classic:** Seated on the floor with one leg straight and one bent in front or back. Reach forward and lock fingers around your foot. Work on lengthening through your back. Hold 10 counts. Do 5x.

Kneeling One Leg Classic      Lying with Raised Leg      Developpe Stretch

---

*Hint*

*When stretching out a muscle, breath out and relax as you stretch. It helps a lot. You can also talk to your stretching muscles telling them to let go and relax.*

# MUSCLES of the Outer Thigh

## MUSCLES CONNECTED TO A THICK BAND OF FASCIA, WHICH OUTWARDLY LIFT AND ROTATE THE LEG

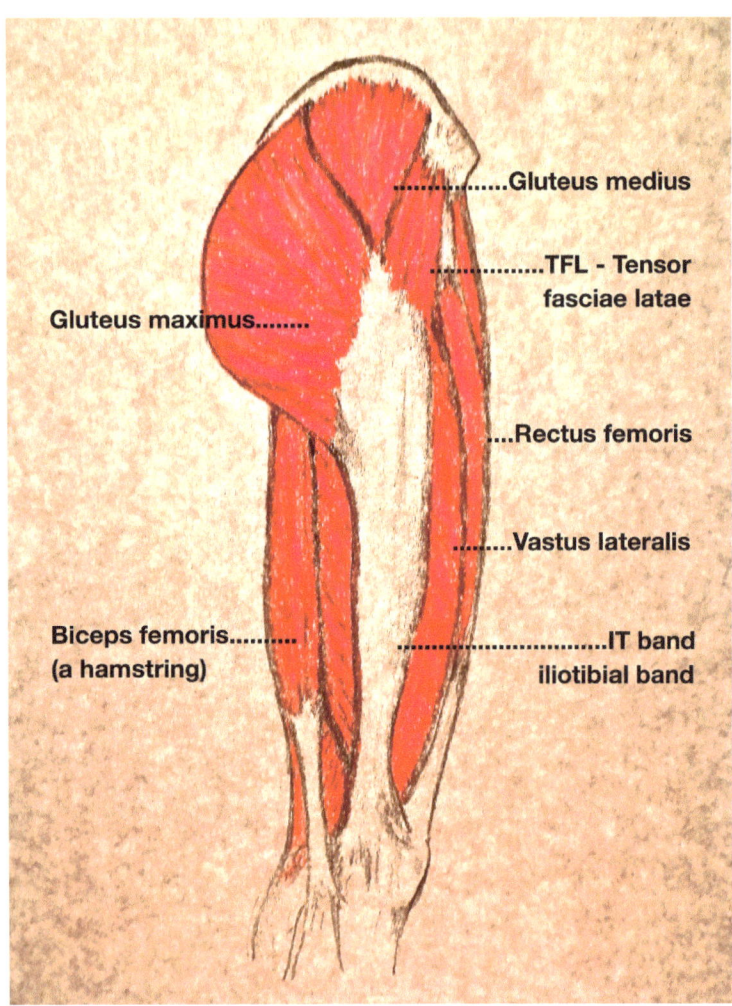

*These muscles, along with the inner thigh, work to stabilize and maintain alignment between your hips and legs holding you upright - especially when standing on one leg.*

### GLUTEALS

**Gluteus maximus** - lifts the leg derrière and supports the pelvis and trunk when standing on one leg.

**Gluteus medius and minimus** - pull the leg out to the side; they also hold the hips stable when standing on one leg and in retiré they help turnout the thigh.

### THE QUADS

**Rectus femoris** - a powerful muscle that extends the knee.

**Vastus Lateralis** - the larger outer thigh muscle which extends and stabilizes the knee.

### TFL

Helps lift the leg to the side when in parallel, stabilizes the knee in développé, and stabilizes the hips when standing on one leg.

### IT Band

A tough sheath of connective fascia running the length of the outer thigh preventing excessive rotation in the leg during movement.

### HAMSTRINGS

**Biceps femoris** - a two-headed muscle which flexes the knee and also lifts the leg derrière as in attitude.

# THE OUTER THIGH Series

**Purpose:** To build strength and stretch the outer thigh.

## *Technique*

Be gentle. Don't jerk your motions when doing stretching or strengthening exercises.

1. Engage your core first.
2. Hold spine in neutral (waist off the floor) with hips and shoulders stacked.
3. Inhale while lifting. Exhale while lowering.
4. Stop if there is any pain in knee or inner groin.
5. Don't do these stretches if you feel pressure in the hip socket.

## Strengthening the Outer Thigh

**Side Lifts:** Whether lying on your side or standing, with or without a resistance band, lift your leg away from center to strengthen your outer thigh.

**Développés in Parallel:** Retiré one leg and plié the other. As you développé to the side, maintain your parallel alignment, and straighten your plié. Legs arrive in full extension at the same time.

## Stretching the Outer Thigh

**The Crossed Leg Twist:** Seated as below, press your opposite elbow on the outside of your bent knee. Keeping your back straight, twist your shoulders and look behind. Press back with your elbow.

**Laying Outer Thigh Stretch:** Lie on back with knees bent and feet on the floor. Lift and turnout one leg placing ankle on knee. Lock hands around the thigh and pull toward your chest.

# MUSCLES in Front of the Thigh

**Powerful muscles which lift the leg in walking, running, and leaping.**

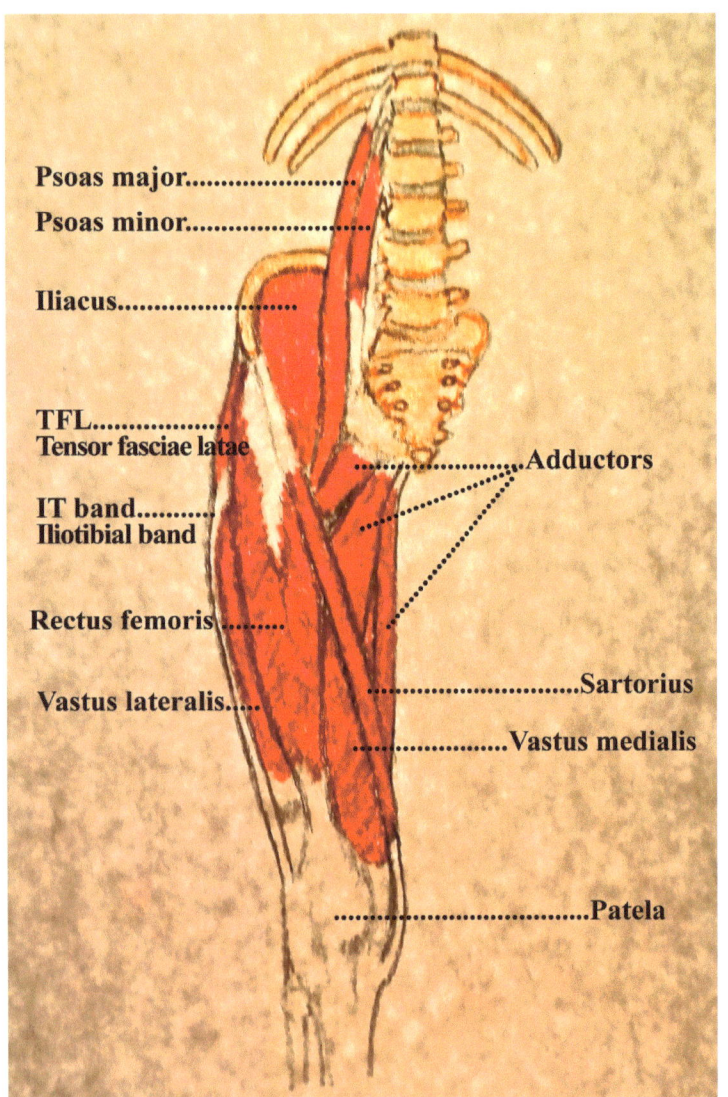

*The quadriceps (quads) meaning, "four-headed muscle, combine to form the strongest muscle in the body, they are essential for walking, running, sauté movements, leaps, and plié. They are also used to flex the leg at the hip. In grand battement and développé, it is important to not rely on the quads for extension as they diminish turnout.*

## ILIOPSOAS

**Psoas major, minor and iliacus** - They flex and turnout the thigh as well as move the lower spine forward.

## THE QUADS

**Rectus Femoris** - A powerful muscle which extends the knee and flexes the leg at the hip.

**Vastus Lateralis** - An outer thigh muscle and the largest quad. It extends and stabilizes the knee.

**Vastus Medialis Oblique - VMO** - A large deep inner thigh muscle that not only stabilizes and extends the lower leg but keeps the knee cap tracking correctly.

**Vastus Intermedius** (not shown) - Lies below the rectus femurs.

## TFL

Helps to raise the leg when in parallel, stabilizes the knee, and helps stabilize the hips when on one leg.

## SARTORIUS

Helps to flex the leg and knee, pull the leg to center and rotate it outward in turnout.

## ADDUCTORS

They work together to pull the thigh toward center as well as help lift and turnout the leg.

## HIP FLEXORS INCLUDE:

Iliopsoas, sartorius, rectus femoris, pectineus, adductors longus and brevis, gracilis and tensor fasciae latae.

# THE QUADRICEPS Series

**Purpose:** Quad stretches are extremely important for knee pain and injury prevention.

## Strengthening the Quads

In ballet, we're not as interested in building quad strength as we are inner thigh strength, for they can take over the work of the weaker inner thigh and hamper turnout. So the following strengthening exercise in turnout will work the VMO (the innermost quad) as well as the inner thigh.

**VMO Lift:** Lying with one leg straight and one bent with knee up and foot on floor. Turnout the straight leg and flex the foot. Press through your heel slowly lifting to the height of your bended knee (5 counts). Point and flex your toe and return in 5 counts.

## Stretching the Quads

**NOTE: Take the time to stretch your quads as well as other muscles after using them intensely. This reduces your risk of injury and muscle soreness.**

Basic Version: Holding your foot in back, press your knee back as far as possible and hold. This is a great stretch to do when your quads are feeling a little tight.

## Perfecting Changements

### The Most Common Faults in Changements

- Pulling the upper body back at the top of your jump.
- Sticking the bottom out in back before and after your jump.
- Rolling in 5th - especially the back foot.
- Lifting the back heel when landing in 5th.
- Plié not deep enough.

**Correct**

**Incorrect**

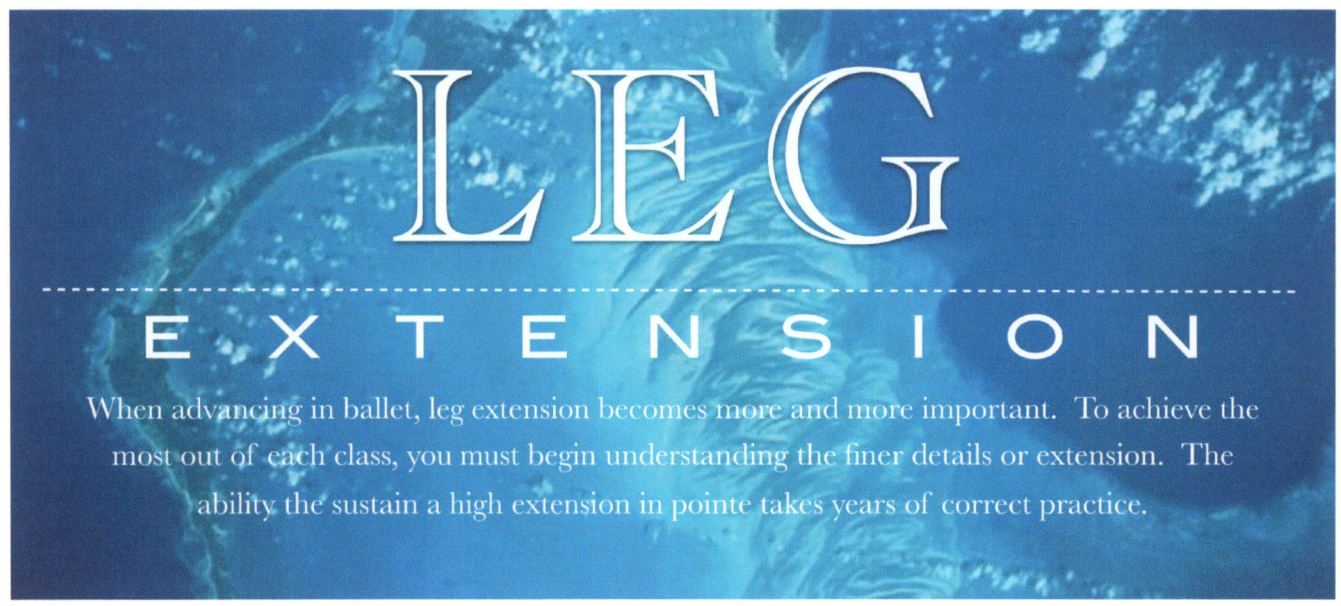

# LEG EXTENSION

When advancing in ballet, leg extension becomes more and more important. To achieve the most out of each class, you must begin understanding the finer details or extension. The ability the sustain a high extension in pointe takes years of correct practice.

## INCREASE STRENGTH IN CORE AND HIP FLEXERS

Every time you do a grand battement or développé, you use your core and back muscles. Work on the strengthening exercises for your TA (transversus abdominis) and Iliopsoas muscles found in the Core and Back chapter particularly on the Core Stability and Plank Series.

## INCREASE FLEXIBILITY IN HIP AND LEGS

Flexibility allows your leg to go higher, but the range of motion around your hip joint determines how high it will go. In grand battement and développés devant, don't attempt a higher extension by allowing your hip to move forward and/or by bending your supporting knee. You will add motion from those joints and your leg will go higher, but you will sacrifice your placement, alignment, and turnout. Twisting the hip forward forces you to use the quads making them stronger thus bulkier and with loss of turnout. Bending the supporting leg makes you look heavy and places your weight back on your heel, not to mention the extra stress on your supporting knee. You don't want any of these, so pull up in your supporting leg and keep your hips square.

## BUILD ENDURANCE IN YOUR MUSCLES

Endurance will hold your leg up. Remember the difference between fast and slow twitch muscles? All muscles have around 50% of both types, some more some less. Building strength is about the force of getting your leg up - a short burst of energy (fast twitch). Endurance is your lasting ability to hold an extension (slow twitch). The following exercises, designed by Lisa Howell, are for building endurance.

# EXTENSION TO ENDURANCE

## EXERCISES TO BUILD ENDURANCE IN EXTENSION

### 2" ON THE LOW BARRE:
*Side to the barre - Développé devant and place leg on barre.*
  Lift your leg 2 inches, hold 5 counts, and lower to barre.
  Repeat as many times as you can.
  Relax and stretch the muscles completely.
  Repeat on other leg, then to the side, then back.

### 2" UP AND DOWN EXTENSION:
*Side to the barre - Développé front.*
  Lower your leg 2 inches, then lift 2 inches.
  Repeat as many times as you can.
  Relax and stretch the muscles completely.
  Repeat on other leg, then to the side, then back.

### MAKE SURE YOUR PLACEMENT IS CORRECT and DON'T STRAIN TOO MUCH.

*When concerned about extension in arabesque, check your mid-back muscle, TA (Transverse abdominis), Hamstrings, and Gluteus maximus for weakness. Any, or all, of these could limit your range. Also, check for tightness in your iliopsoas.*

**BACK EXTENSION:** For dancers having trouble with pinching in your back:

*Stand at a corner barre and place your hands on the barre or wall in front of you.*
Développé to arabesque derrière and check your placement.

Make sure your shoulder (the same side as your lifted leg) is not pulling back. Pulling your shoulder back not only pinches your back but encourages your hip to lift and twist off your supporting leg. Lengthen your back and engage your core, as sitting into your back also creates pinching.

Place your foot on the barre letting your leg rest. Stretch your back long, and lift your leg as high as it can go. Feel your butt muscles holding your leg.

  Now do Test One. Only **after** you can do Test One comfortably move on to Test Two.

# EXTENSION TESTS

## Test I

*Stand at the barre:*

**Développé** your leg devant, à la seconde or derrière onto the barre.

**Lift** your leg off the barre 1 inch without letting your back work or move in any direction. **One inch only.**

**Hold 5 counts,** feeling which muscles are working.

**Place your leg** back on the barre.

**Do 10x**. Gradually working up to 20x.

## Test II

*Stand at the barre:*

**Demi-plié,** maintaining a straight back. If needed, you can bend slightly forward at the hips, but keep your shoulders upright.

**Lift** the leg just off the barre without rolling your plié inward.

**Straighten** your plié holding the lifted leg in position.

**Do** this as many times as you can.

**EXTENSION EXERCISES ARE VERY RIGOROUS!**

Do them 2x a week but not two days in a row. Do them after your class when you will be warmed up.

Although hip alignment must adjust, sacrifice only what is necessary for your extension, as a raised hip pulls you off center.

**Because tension leads to poor muscle tone and loss of strength, be sure to stretch all muscles, especially the iliopsoas, and relax after each of these exercises.**

# FRONT EXTENSION ERRORS

## All too often dancers make terrible technical errors in attempting to reach their highest extension.

### Développés or Grands Battements Devant

Technique in these lovely movements is, all to often, sacrificed for the sake of extension. Train yourself to avoid the following:

- Collapsing the supporting knee.
- Pushing the working hip forward.
- Pulling back on the supporting heel.

Collapsing the supporting knee is often accompanied by a rolling ankle and pronated knee, placing the knee in a very damaging position. Dancers must learn to pull tall, away from the supporting leg, and keep their weight forward on the ball of their foot.

A working hip, which is allowed to move forward, forces the quads to takeover thus sacrificing turnout and placing an unwanted workload on them; The opposite of what a dancer is trying to achieve.

*Incorrect: Supporting leg released, working hip forward, loss of turnout, and pulling back off center.*

*Correct: Hips and shoulders aligned with back and supporting leg stretched.*

# SIDE EXTENSION ERRORS

## Grands Battements or Développés à la Seconde

### Incorrect:
- Working hip is thrown outward and upward.
- Pushing weight back off the ball of the foot onto the heel losing center.
- Back tilting or moving.

Hip alignment in the working leg is often sacrificed for extension. Not only does throwing the working hip up and out pull your hips out of alignment, but it pulls weight onto your heel and away from the barre. This action, when done repeatedly, also places added stress on the supporting hip joint.

### Correct:
- Core engaged.
- Hips and shoulders square.
- Piriformis area muscles engaged and held on both sides.
- 60/40 weight distribution maintained.
- Back lifted and held erect.

*Incorrect: Lifting leg from back of hip forces quads to work harder and loses turnout and centering.*

*Correct: Working the right muscles allows the leg to lift from front of hip and thigh and retains turnout and centering.*

# BACK EXTENSION ERRORS

## Grands Battements or Développés Derrière

### Errors:

- Pulling back in shoulder off the working leg.
- Raising the hip.
- Shifting weight back on the heel.
- Raised the leg not behind shoulder.

Pulling back in the shoulder pinches the waistline together and pulls the shoulders out of alignment. Instead lengthen through your waist, stretch out of your hips, and keep your shoulders square.

Raising the hip also pinches at the waist and twists the hips out of alignment placing inward pressure on the supporting leg.

Rocking back on your heel shifts your weight behind you forcing you to pull on the barre for balance and does not allow you to elevé without shifting your weight back onto the ball.

*Incorrect: Hip raised and shoulder pulled backward causing pinching in back.*

*Correct: Back stretched long with shoulders and hips aligned.*

**Try testing your center by lifting your hand slightly off the barre when doing grand battements or développés.**

# EXTENSION AND CORE

## Because the core is vital to extension, do the following exercises before and after your extension work.

### Abdominal Strengthening: Before extension work

Lie on your back holding a small rolled towel under your neck with knees bent. Crunch up, lifting only your head and shoulders (not your back) in 10 *very, very slow* counts. Return in 10, *very, very slow* counts, but don't relax! Repeat twice more before you rest. Keep breathing.

**Alternative for Towel:** Place one hand behind your neck and reach the other hand toward your knees.

### Psoas Stretches: After extension work

Repeated flexing of the psoas muscles in extension work can leave them strained and shortened with tension. Always stretch the psoas out to relieve this tension with either of the stretches shown below.

**Lunge in Parallel:** Step into a forward lunge, pull up through the abs and press gently forward feeling a stretch in front of the hip of back leg.

**Runners' Lunge, a deeper stretch:** As above with back knee to floor and hands in 2nd, pull up through the back and stretch the psoas by pressing forward through the hip. Twisting your torso away from the back leg will stretch the TFL.

# EXTENSION AND STANDING LEG

It's a common myth that grand battement or développé (in any direction), comes only from the working leg. This makes our efforts focus only on the working leg. In reality, however, it's the standing leg that allows the working leg to be lifted. Put more energy into lengthening your standing leg and the working leg will be free to do its job.

### Beginning a Grand Battement or Développé:

- Hold your standing leg with the ankle pulled up balancing 60/40.
- Lengthen through the knee.
- Turnout in the supporting hip.
- Lengthen the back.
- Keep your hips square.

*Don't twist, buckle, or tilt this placement as the working leg lifts.*

### Executing a Développé Devant or a la Seconde:

Concentrate on the lengthening and turning out your standing leg.

- Pass through a well-placed, turned-out retiré.
- Développé by pressing your knee back and heel outward to attitude.
- Extend fully without dropping your leg.

### Executing a Développé Derrière:

Concentrate on the lengthening and turning out your standing leg.

- As you stretch into attitude, lead with the knee.
- Place your knee directly behind your shoulder as you unfold your leg.
- Keep your toe level with the knee unless your attitude is higher than your hip.
- Stretch your leg fully to the back.

**NOTE: Too many dancers don't stretch their legs in back leaving them slightly bent.**

Over time you will strengthen the correct muscles and achieve higher, more correctly placed grand battements and développés. It takes time and effort.

# KNEES
## HYPOEXTENDED

There are two basic reasons for hypoextention in the knees. First is lacking the proper strength to keep the knees straight. Second, is that the knee is restricted in the tendons, ligaments or the muscles which hold it, or even partially due to the bone-joint structure itself.

### TEST #1

**Purpose:** Finding your knee's range

**Test:** Sit down and relax. Have a teacher, parent or a friend bend and straighten one knee at a time. If the results show an adequate range, you simply lack the strength you need to hold your knees straight. *(NOTE: It is much harder to keep your knee straight when standing on one leg and doing a grand battement extension than when simply standing.)* Should your legs not be able to extend to neutral you have hypoextended knees.

### TEST #2

**Purpose:** If your test shows weakness, test your VMO's strength.

**Exercise:** Sit on the floor with your legs straight out front. Pull your knee cap up and feel your VMO muscle located on the top inside of your knee. Weakness here could be the answer. Many dancers who are hypoextended have weakness here. "When this happens, over time, the knee will become stiffer as it is never going into its full range," writes Lisa Howell.

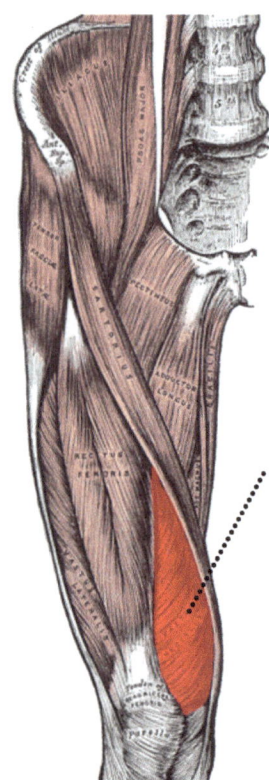

VMO - the innermost muscle of the quads.

**Tests are from the writings of Lisa Howell.**

# HYPOEXTENDED KNEES

## TEST #3

**Purpose:** If a dancer does not have full range in Test #1, she needs to find out where the blockage is located.

**Feeling the Restriction:** Where do you "feel" the restriction when trying to straighten your knee - back / front / either side / deep inside? Finding the location gives us a place to start.

- **A. BACK OF THE KNEE:** A little muscle named 'Popliteus' can block extension range if it is too tight. Because there are many delicate nerves and blood vessels there, dancers should not take it upon themselves to massage this area, but a qualified physical therapist should know how to relieve the tension in this muscle. Lisa Howell explained, "I have had some extraordinary results with some students by doing this."

- **B. INSIDE THE KNEE:** Stiffness here can also be helped with massage to the inner thigh muscles. Long smooth strokes along the inner thigh, from the knee up can improve flexibility not only in the knee but in center splits.

- **C. TENSION DOWN THE BACK OF THE LEG:** Especially if the dancer has started to grow. Foot and calf massage as well as the Piriformis Release with a tennis ball is also recommended.

- **D. ADDITIONAL MASSAGE:** Massage in the gap between the inner and outer hamstrings to release both fascial and neural tension. This has made a big difference in many dancers.

"If none of these appear to be the cause of the restriction, then it may be that the ligaments on the inside of the knee are blocking the range. I do not advocate stretching the ligaments in the knees in any form as this usually leads to many other problems. Do not put any force through the knees to try to straighten them out as I have seen some very dangerous techniques! Any releases or stretches need to be well thought out and aimed to slowly increase a dancer's range and strength over time," advised Ms. Howell.

## EXERCISE #1

**Purpose:** Strengthening the VMO.

**Exercise:** Seated with legs extended, knees straight, and heels on floor. Tighten your thigh muscles for 10 sec. Release and relax 3 sec. Do 10x.

## EXERCISE #2

**Purpose:** Stretch the hamstrings.

**Exercise:** Seated with one leg extended and one bent. Reach hands to heel of extended leg and bend forward as far as possible. Hold 10 sec. Release and repeat. Do 5x on each side.

# KNEES
## HYPEREXTENTION

*"If not controlled, hyperextended knees can cause trauma to the knee capsule and eventually can cause strain or even tearing of the ligaments behind the knee. It may also place stress on the lower leg which could lead to shin splints and in extreme cases could lead to a tibial stress fracture. When the knee goes back into hyperextention the thigh bone (femur) tends to rotate inward & feet tend to roll in."*
Lisa Howell

## MUSCLES AND HYPEREXTENTION

When looking at the x-ray of a hyperextended knee. You can understand how overstretched the tendons and ligaments are behind the knee. Overstretched ligaments and tendons are usually accompanied by changes in adjacent muscle groups, including the soleus muscle.

## SOLEUS STRETCHING

If the soleus is short and tight, it will pull the upper ends of the tibia and fibula backward, contributing to hyperextension. It is important for dancers with hyperextended knees to do Soleus Stretches often and on a regular basis.

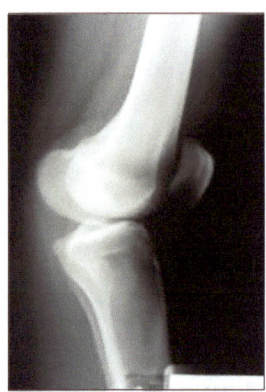

**Hyperextended Knee x-ray**

## QUADRICEPS STRENGTHENING

Hyperextended dancers usually have weak quadriceps or don't engage them when standing. Instead they rest back in their knee joints. To overcome this habit, dancers need to strengthen and activate their quads in all straight-knee positions.

## POSTURE PROBLEMS

A greater posture problem is created as the knees curve back, the pelvis tilts forward, the chest collapses back, and the head juts forward. These shift compensations not only add to knee problems but lower back and neck pain as well. Managing hyperextention goes hand in hand with creating a spacious, vertical posture.

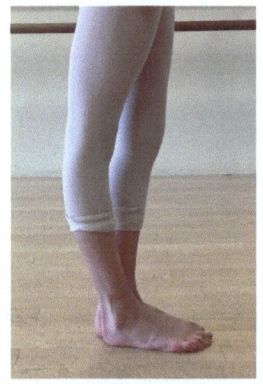

**Hyperextended**

## MANAGING HYPEREXTENTION

First, find neutral by moving the top of your tibia (your large lower leg bone) forward so it is straight below your femur (your upper leg bone). Memorize this feeling and hold your knees in this position every time you are standing. At the same time, work on your core and posture placement. Constantly remind yourself to "Stand Tall" and soon it will be automatic.

# HYPEREXTENSION

**Hyperextended joints are due to the looseness of the tendons and ligaments.**

"So many dancers have hyperextended knees," says Emily Sandow, a physical therapist at the Hospital for Joint Diseases in New York City. "What's important is how you use the hyperextension, how you control it."

Strengthen the muscles which support your knee so you won't drop back into hyperextension. "Dancers—especially ballet dancers—don't like to have bulky muscles," she says. They tend to hang out in their ligaments and rely on them to hold them up.

Since dancers are overstretched already, you really don't want to rely on your ligaments too much. Sandow recommends students keep their quads "gently active" to hold the tibia in line and prevent pushing back in the knee joint. It will help to strengthen the quads and hamstrings. Dancers with hyperextended legs have to retrain their legs. At first they feel like they are bending their knees all the time.

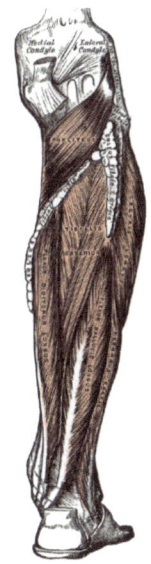

Sandow said, "You also have a little muscle called 'Popliteus' that sits across the back of the knee. This muscle is designed to unlock your knee from full extension, but if the knee is constantly overstretched, it can get a little inflamed and become sore if you really stretch your knees in class.

However, bending the knees also has its drawbacks… Working with the knees bent can result in excessive tension in the quadriceps (front of thigh) and a build-up of muscle bulk (as can over straightening!).

The trick is to develop an awareness of 'pulling up' not 'pulling back' when you straighten your legs.

When you have hypermobile joints, it is very important to learn how to not only control your joint in neutral, but to recover when your knee does go into hyperextension.

The biggest challenge is actually doing this in class. If you have hyperextended knees, it will feel very strange to stand in first with the heels together, so try having a maximum of one inch between your heels, at first, and focus on maintaining control through your knees. This is especially important when you begin to take one foot off the floor.

While it takes some effort to manage hyperextended knees, once you have developed the strength to control the placement of your knee in any position, you will not only have the skill and protection from risk of injury proper placement gives, but the beauty of a lovely line for classical dance!

See exercises as recommended by Lisa Howell on the following page.

# HYPEREXTENDED KNEE EXERCISES

## Why Find Neutral?

Hyperextension leaves the back of the knees vulnerable, though, when held in neutral, dancers feel that their knees are bent. The challenge is, not only to build strength in the muscles surrounding and stabilizing the knee, but to constantly work on holding neutral knee placement in every dance class as well as throughout the day. After awhile the habit of holding your knees straight will start to feel natural.

## EXERCISE #1

**Purpose:** To feel the proper placement of your knees.

**Exercise:** Do with either one or both legs. Sit on the floor with legs straight in front. Slowly hyperextend your knees, lifting your heels as high as possible. Lower your heels until just off the floor ( ¼ inch ) lengthening from hip socket to heel. Hold this position for at least 10 sec.

## EXERCISE #2

**Purpose:** Gaining control in front and behind center.

**Exercise:** Same position as above. Lift heel ¼ inch off the floor. Straighten, moving the heel higher then lower — again to ¼ inch. Repeat doing in little pulses. Do 20x.

## EXERCISE #3

**Purpose:** To feel correct placement of knees when standing.

**Exercise:** Repeat Exercise #1 standing first in parallel on both legs then in 1st with less turnout than in class. When strong enough, repeat on one leg and do the following:

- Control the knees into a tiny plié, and return to neutral.
- Hyperextend the knees a tiny bit, and return to neutral.
  Maintain pull up throughout. Do at least 10x - 4x/day.

# BOW LEGS vs. KNOCK KNEES

## BOW LEGS

Legs are labeled bowed when standing with feet together, instead of touching, the knees bow away from each other. It is quite common in toddlers under 18 months. but walking usually corrects this condition by age 3.

## STRAIGHTENING BOW LEGS

Exercises to straighten bowed legs consist of strengthening the muscles surrounding the knee and upper thigh. This is why ballet is such a positive influence for not only bow-legged children but knock-kneed ones as well. The emphasis on turnout, lift, placement, inner thigh strengthening as well as total leg and foot control can do wonders for straightening or at least managing the legs.

## KNOCK KNEES

Knock knees come together at the knee and splay out at the feet. They are usually accompanied by rolling ankles. This, as with bow legs, causes uneven weight distribution within the knees and the probability of chronic knee pain in later life. Also, being over- weight adds a lot of stress on the knees. Curiously, doctors recommend the same exercises for both knock knees and bow legs. I'm a firm believer in the benefits ballet plays in both bow legs and knock knees. Not only am I a prime example, (having been placed in ballet for knock-knees and rolling ankles) but several adult dancers have told me that it was ballet that straightened their legs.

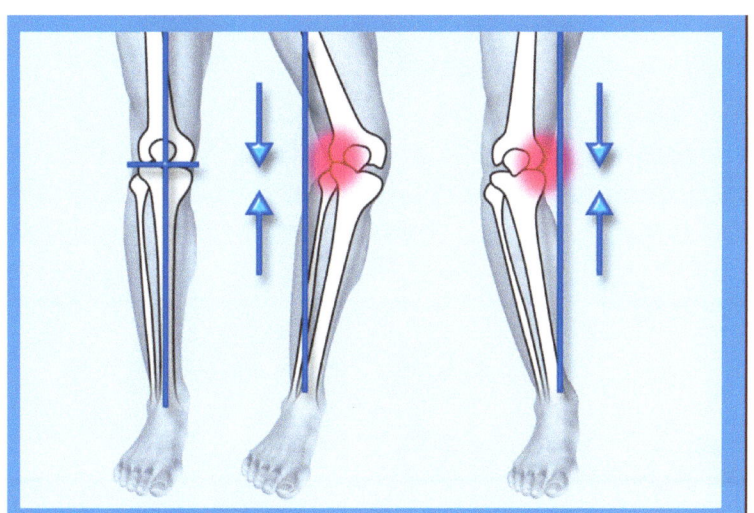

*Weight distribution on the knees*

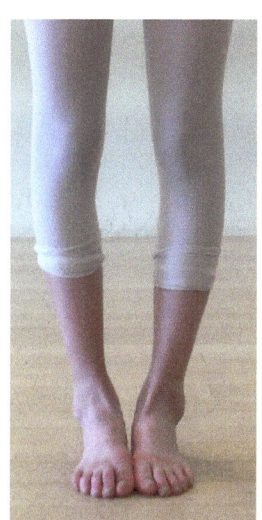

*Bow Legs*

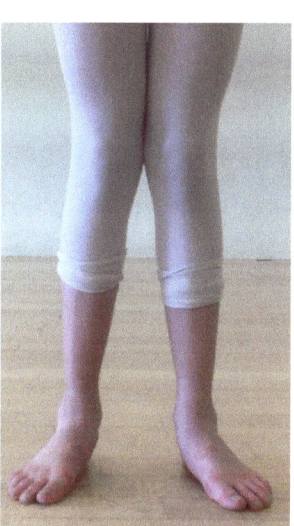

*Knock Knees*

# ASSESSMENTS #9 - #14

## #9 and #10 - 20 Elevés on One Leg

**Purpose:** To demonstrate foot, ankle and lower leg strength in a single leg stand.

**Errors:** Unable to do 20 elevés slowly on each leg - not rising fully to demi-pointe—rolling off your point of balance—clenched or clawed toes.

**Correction:** A strength issue: Muscles of the foot, ankle and calf lack strength enough to raise the body 20 times up to a full demi-pointe. Do lots of elevés on a step daily.

## #11 and #12 - Changements

**Purpose:** Demonstrating core control as well as foot and ankle strength with the ability to spring into the air without disturbing your alignment.

**Errors:** In the air: Core releases and shoulders pull back.

In 5th Plié: Back foot rolls—knees roll forward—poor 5th—bottom sticks out.

**Correction:** A foot, ankle or core strength issue. Muscles under the foot are not strong enough to hold instep strong. Pulling shoulders back by not controlling the core and trying to lift from the back. More attention to foot placement in 5th. Strengthen and/or open turnout in landing. Work on core strengthening and torso placement.

## #13 and #14 - Single Leg Stand w/ Plié

**Purpose:** To demonstrate foot, ankle and lower leg control and balance when on one leg in plié.

**Errors:** Tendons on the top and side of foot and ankle flick off and on, foot wobbles and/or toes claw or clench.

**Correction:** A strength issue. Muscles under the foot are not strong enough to hold the instep strong. Flicking tendons are the bodies attempt to hold balance from the top of the foot.

### Working More Effectively in Class:

- Hold the barre only with the tips of your fingers. This avoids relying on the barre for balance and forces you to find center.
- Use your feet strongly all the time. Do articulated tendus both in barre and center floor work.
- With each jump, use your feet strongly during takeoffs and landings.
- Feel the balancing points of your foot on the floor and use the small intrinsic muscles to hold your foot firmly.

# KNEES AND LEGS Assessments #9 - #14

| ASSESSMENTS | REQUIREMENTS TO PASS |
|---|---|
| **#9 and #10**<br>**20 Single Leg Elevés** | Hold a wall or barre in a single leg stand with posture held in neutral and knee straight. Elevé to full demi-pointe taking 5 counts to rise and 5 counts to lower. Build up to 20x and be sure you stretch out your calf afterward. "Elevé on a Step" will strengthen the feet and calf for this test. |
| **#11 and #12**<br>**Changements** | Demi-plié with your back held straight and knees well turned out. When you spring into the air, don't allow your shoulders to pull back. Hold arms softly with no tension and stretch your feet to a full pointe. Change feet in the air and land in a strong 5th holding your demi-plié with back straight, both ankles lifted, and knees opened out over your toes. |
| **#13 and #14**<br>**Single Leg Stand w/ Plié** | Stand in parallel on one foot in plié without wobbling, clenching, clawing, or flicking tendons. To improve this assessment, you must strengthen the muscles beneath your feet as described previously. Rely on the strength of your foot muscles to keep you steady, not from the muscles of the lower leg. |

# LEG PAIN

## SHIN SPLINTS (TIBIAL STRESS SYNDROME)

We can all have shin splints at one time or another. They cause a throbbing, aching feeling in your shins. While they often heal on their own, severe shin splints can hamper your ability to walk around (let alone dance) and may need a doctor's care.

*They can be caused from:*

- *Overuse of adjoining muscles* causing irritated and swollen muscles.
- *Uncontrolled landings* - not using toe, ball, heel, plié in your feet and knees.
- *Rolling ankles or "flat feet"* - when the impact of landing a jump causes the arch of your foot to collapse, stressing muscles and tendons in your foot, ankle and shin.
- *Insufficiently warming up* before running or strenuous activity as in allegro work. NOTE: Toe taps before such an exertion will warm up the shins.
- *Dancing on hard surfaces* such as concrete or asphalt.

*Should you develop shin splints, follow the care program below:*

- *Ice the shin* to reduce pain and swelling. Do it for 20-30 minutes every three to four hours for two to three days, or until the pain is gone.
- *Anti-inflammatory painkillers*. Non-steroidal anti-inflammatory drugs like ibuprofen or aspirin will help with pain and swelling. However, they should only be used occasionally unless your doctor says otherwise.
- *Arch supports for your shoes.* Orthotics should be used only as a temporary measure for flat feet until the foot muscles gain strength necessary to support the instep.
- *Stretching exercises* to stretch out the front of the ankle and shin.
- *A sleeve or wrap* to support and warm the lower leg. After healing, leg warmers can help keep the lower leg warm during class.
- *Exercises/massage* to strengthen muscles in your shins, feet, and ankles.

## CHRONIC PATELLAR TENDONITIS

Often called "jumper's knee," this condition is the inflammation of the tendon and area's surrounding the knee, usually due to overuse, especially jumping. A sharp abrupt muscle contraction or stretch can cause pain which increases with continued activity. Chronic tendonitis can often take place with increased activity on an overused tendon. Symptoms show swelling or bruising along with local tenderness and pain.

## POPLITEUS

A little muscle behind the knee designed to unlock hyperextension. If it is constantly over stretched it can become inflamed and painful. Home treatment for these two conditions include ice, elevation, and rest to prevent further damage with a gradual return to activities. The area can be wrapped for support. Any sharp sudden pain or prolonged pain needs to be seen by your doctor or specialist.

## PATELLAR TRACKING DISORDER - see your doctor

This is when the kneecap shifts out of place as the leg bends or straightens, usually moving to the outside of the leg.

The kneecap, lined with cartilage, is held in place by a tendon on top and a ligament on the bottom. If the grove between the leg bones and kneecap is too shallow, the cartilage is damaged, or the tissue holding it is too loose or tight, the kneecap can shift off track. The VMO's strength is incredibly important in keeping the kneecap in line. With a dedicated strengthening program, there is no reason you can't eliminate this problem.

## CHRONIC PATELLAR TENDONITIS

In a study of exercises, the eccentric squat resulted in signifigantly lowering pain and produced twice as many "pain free" subjects at the end of the trial than a group not doing this exercise.

## ECCENTRIC SQUAT

Balance on the upper portion of a 25° decline board in parallel on one leg. Plié in 3 counts (eccentric phase). Straighten on 4 (concentric phase). Do 15x with a 10 sec. Rest and repeat 2 more times.

## VMO STRENGTHENING EXERCISES

SEATED on a chair with feet on the floor. Place a softball between your knees. Squeeze ball with your thighs and hold 5 counts. Do 10-20x, 2x/day.

LYING on your back with a pillow bending your knees to 30 degrees. Squeeze a soft ball as above and straighten the weak knee squeezing and holding 5 counts. Do 10-20x, 2x/day.

STANDING with back against the wall and feet parallel 2nd about 4 inches from the wall. Squeeze ball as above and slowly plié down holding 5 counts. Do 10-20x, 2x/day.

# Osgood-Schlatter
## disease/syndrome

Osgood-Schlatter disease is not really a disease but an inflammation of the patella's tendon where it inserts into the shin bone. It is probably the most common cause of knee pain in active children between the age of 9 to 16.

Symptoms show swelling and tenderness to the touch. Indication of a problem is rubbing the top of your shin or needing to ice your lower knee in or after class.

Bones can grow more quickly during certain periods in a young dancer's life. This can cause the area where the tendon attaches to become inflamed.

Also, besides this inflammation, small fractures can occur.

At this union, a small piece of bone can pull away from the tibia (the shin bone) causing extra bone growth to occur and create a painful bump.

There is, however, a lot that can be done to minimize the pain produced by this condition, preventing the bump from developing, and get back to dancing as soon as possible.

Much of this condition can come from tension in the muscles around the hip and knee.

Stretches and releases are important in correcting any lower leg technique that can cause an excessive load on the knees such as rolling knees in during plié. Sufferers often have weakness in their hips and core.

**NOTE: This condition usually takes care of itself as growing settles down.**

| 3 Main Causes | Is There Pain During: | Treatment - RICE + T |
|---|---|---|
| • Children between the ages of 9 and 16<br>• Involved in high-level physical activity<br>• During a "growth spurt" | • Running<br>• Plié / squatting<br>• Sautés / jumps / leaps<br>• Especially walking up or down stairs | • Rest<br>• Ice<br>• Compression<br>• Elevation + Taping |

# TEARS INSIDE of the Knee

## MENISCUS TEARS

The inside of our knee has two "C"-shaped rubbery cartilage pieces called meniscus; one at the outside, and the other at the inside edge of our knee. They serve to steady our knees by balancing our weight across our knees as well as cushion our leg bones from rubbing together.

### THREE TYPES OF MENISCUS TEARS

**A minor tear:** Slight pain and swelling that usually goes away in two or three weeks.

**A moderate tear:** Pain at the side or center of the knee with swelling and getting worse in the second and third days. The knee can feel stiff, but walking is usually possible. A sharp pain might be felt in the knee or when doing plié. These symptoms will go away after a couple weeks, but can return if the knee is overused.

**A severe tear:** When a meniscus is torn badly, it can shift into the knee joint making it catch, pop or lock up with the pain and swelling. It may also become stiff immediately or within a few days. It could feel wobbly, give way without warning, or you may not be able to even straighten it. **SEE YOUR DOCTOR**

### CAUSES

A meniscus tear can happen from a quick twist or turn. As in landing badly from a leap, with your foot and knee rolling in and the rest of your falling out. A technique tip to remember: Never plant your feet in a 180° turnout and then straighten your knees. This action twists your leg bones in opposite directions putting pressure on the meniscus. Turnout is always from the hip.

## MCL (MEDIAL COLLATERAL LIGAMENT) TEARS

The MCL is the inner ligament of your knee. It stabilizes your knee preventing it from moving side to side.

### TYPES OF MCL TEARS

**A mild or grade 1 injury:** usually getting better in 1 to 3 weeks. May only need home treatment.

**A moderate or grade 2 injury:** usually improves in a month. A knee brace may be needed.

**A severe or grade 3 injury:** may require a hinged brace for a few months with limited weight for 4 to 6 weeks. **SEE YOUR DOCTOR.**

### CAUSES

Like the meniscus tear, a tear in the MCL is caused from a sudden twist in your knee usually from a bad landing or a twist.

# Chapter 4

## ASSESSMENTS 15 - 22

## *Hips and Turnout*

Turnout: The outward rotation of the legs from the hips thus allowing greater extension and ease of motion. It's the foundation of all classical ballet movements and an essential part of its technique.

# SUMMARY
## Chapter 4
# HIPS AND TURNOUT

Turnout is a major factor in ballet but, for most, it doesn't come easily. It takes time, work, and attention to achieve. Discover where your turnout muscles are, and how to use them. Then diligently activate them throughout class. Never, never, never place your feet in 180° turnout position in plié and then straighten knees! This forces your knees to take the turnout which your hips are unable to achieve. This is extremely damaging to a joint that is not designed to twist.

## MUSCLES TO USE IN TURNOUT:

3 groups of muscles plus 1 single muscle turnout your legs:

1. SHORT ROTATORS (piriformis group): 6 muscles in the back of the hip.
2. ADDUCTORS: 4 muscles inside the thigh.
3. ILIOPSOAS: 3 muscles located in front of the pelvis.
4. SARTORIUS (the only single muscle): a long slender muscle attaching to the inner knee and extending up and out to the hip bone.

Find these muscles by placing your fingers on the area they are located and feel them as they activate. Try this with and without turnout. Remember, these muscles are working hard to turn you out, give them a good stretch after class.

## MUSCLES NOT TO USE IN TURNOUT:

1. IN FRONT OF THE HIPS: Using the TFL or rectus femoris (the top center quad) at the front of the hip restricts turnout and can become tight causing stiffness and pain.
2. IN BACK OF THE HIPS: Grabbing with your gluteus maximus actually restricts turnout. Instead, activate your short rotator muscles.

# The **TURNOUT** Muscles

### Short or Lateral Rotator Muscles
The Piriformis, along with other smaller muscles, are located in the lower back of the pelvis.

### Adductors
A group of 4 muscles located on the inside of the femur. Their main actions are to pull the legs together and rotate the femur outward.

### Iliopsoas
Three muscles located deep inside the front of the abdomen are the hip flexors, together known as the iliopsoas, they are the Iliacus, Psoas Major, and Minor.

### Sartorius *(not shown below)*
The sartorius, longest muscle in the body, attaches to the outside of the pelvic crest, runs down the front of the thigh, and inserts on the inside of the lower knee. It helps flex the leg and knee and outwardly rotate the thigh. It uses all of these functions in front attitude.

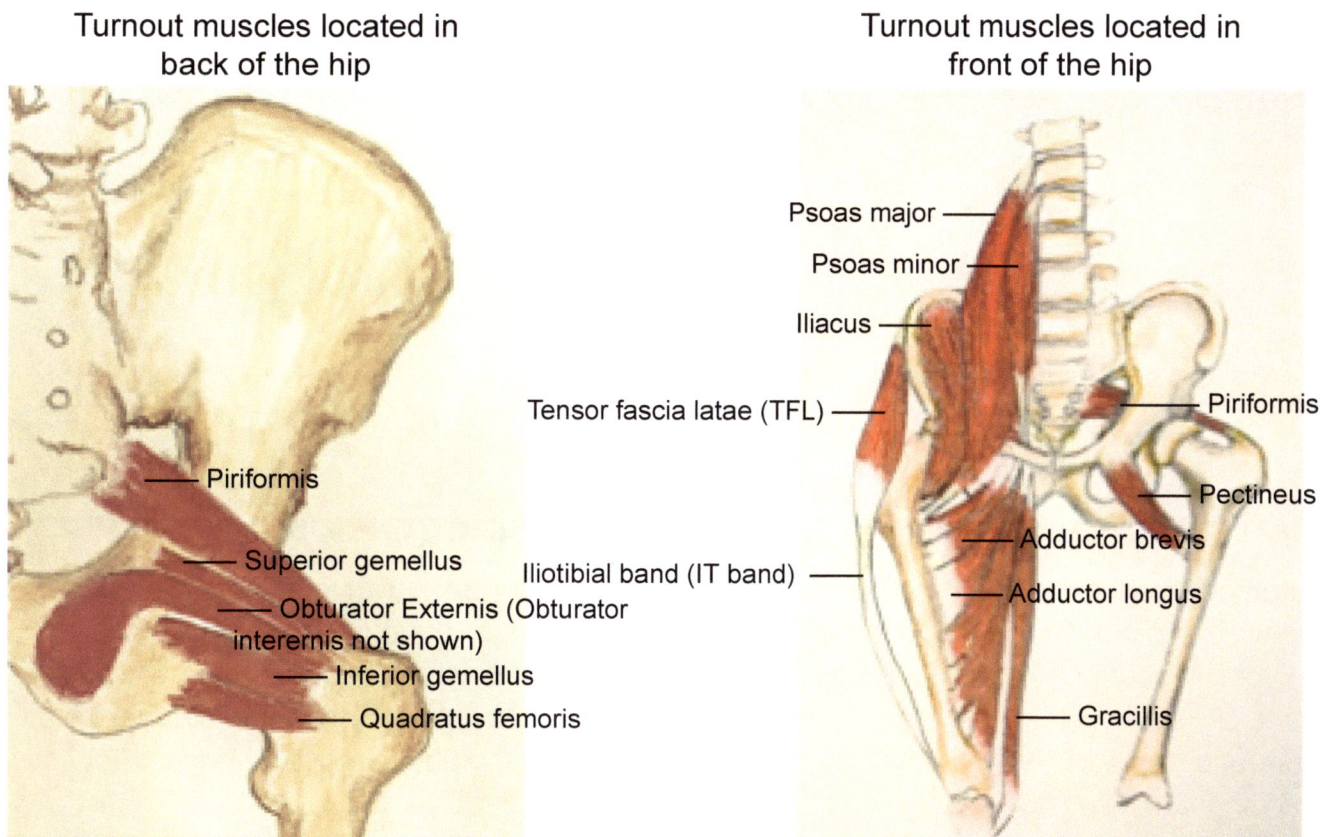

# What DETERMINES My Turnout?

## How much turnout do I have?
## How much do I use?

**TURNOUT IS DETERMINED BY:**

- The bony shape of your pelvis.
- The ligaments that hold your hips together.
- The muscle flexibility around your hips.

**YOUR ILIOFEMORAL LIGAMENT**

As well as the bony structure of your hips, the elasticity of the ligaments holding these bones together is also an important part of your reachable turnout.

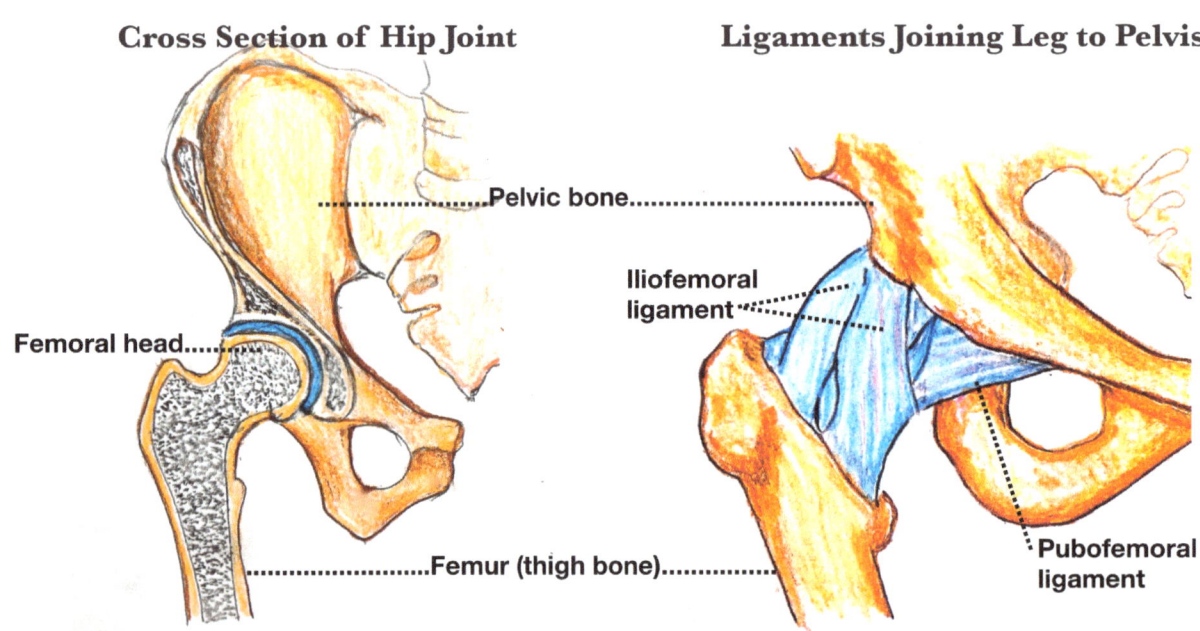

**CAN I STRETCH MY HIPS?**

Stretching can somewhat influence the bony structure of your hips around age 11, before your bones and ligaments are generally set. Muscles, including those that surround your hips, are the only thing you can change at any age.

**RELEASING TENSION IN YOUR HIP**

Lie on your back with knees bent. Place a tennis ball on the outside of your tail bone and gently roll it around your bottom until you feel an area that is tight. Hold on that point for 5 to 10 counts, or until the pain releases. Repeat on the other side.

# DEVELOPING Turnout

A turnout of 180° should not be attempted by beginners. Instead a dancer must build up the strength and flexibility needed to attain this goal. Forcing turnout through the feet and knees will distort the body's alignment and can result in injury, especially in the knee. An angle of 100° will work the muscles in the hip and thigh without causing the knees to rotate inwards and the ankles to "roll over."

In ballet we're expected to hold a 180° turnout of our legs at all times while executing ballet movements. Perfect turnout is rarely attainable at the first attempt and one should not try dancing when overextending one's turnout.

Turnout is natural for some, but for others it needs to be achieved with the greatest of care. Starting young, before the bones are ossified, is usually the best way. Below are other healthy ways to achieve your best turnout in class work.

## Strengthening Turnout Muscles
1. Turnout in Retiré 2. Wall Press 3. Clam Series and Kneeling Clam (same but on hands and knees).

## Stretching Your Turnout Muscles
**Wall Stretch:** Lie on the floor with legs up the wall and bottom against it. Lower your legs in 2nd toward the floor.

**Center Split Stretch:** An advanced stretch is the center splits with your stomach to the ground. It offers maximum turnout stretching potential. Hold this stretch for a while, but stretch only to the point of comfort — no more. Then roll forward moving your legs behind you.

## Movements in the Ballet Class Which Improve Turnout
**Grand Plié:** Open your knees as far as possible, keeping them over your toes throughout your plié. Never, never, never demi-plié and place your feet in a 180° turnout and then straighten your knees!

**Battement Tendu and Battement Degagé:** Work your turnout both in opening and closing movements.

**Rond de Jambe:** This is ballet's primary exercise for turnout. Make good use of each movement by opening both thighs in each position you move through by activating your turnout muscles throughout the entire combination.

**Développé and Grand Battements Devant:** The inner thigh muscles play a major role in properly executing these movements. Especially active is the sartorius and the piriformis muscle group (piriformis, gemellus, obturators, gluteus minimus) as well as the adductors. Be careful not to rely on the quads in a développé or grand battement devant. If you allow your working hip to go up and forward for the sake of extension, your quads will take over reducing your turnout.

**Développé and Grand Battement à la seconde:** Using the inner thigh à la seconde is also necessary for turnout and the same care in not relying on the quads still holds.

**Développé and Grand Battement Derrière:** Your turnout derrière relies particularly on the piriformis muscle group and lengthening your iliopsoas. Don't forget to turnout your supporting leg! Focus on contracting the quadratus femoris muscle for turnout on one leg. (Shown in "Turnout Muscles Located in Front of the Hip" diagram.)

# Points of **RESTRICTION**

Lisa Howell tells us, "The truth is... Most of us have the capacity for a lot more turnout than we currently have, or are using. All it takes is a little education, a little understanding, and a little exploration, to start on the path to much happier hips!" She notes the following:

"Once you have found your true turnout muscles, and can use them well in class, you will feel your turnout naturally increasing. This is because you will not be using so much force to turnout and less tension develops in all the other muscles around the hips. Try avoiding strong stretches, especially forcing the legs out into second. It is OK to feel a stretch in the inner thigh, but if there is pain or stretching in the front of the hip, then it is best to avoid that position."

## WHERE ARE YOUR EXACT RESTRICTION POINTS?

When you're in the frog stretch, a grande plié, center splits, or simply standing in 5th, close your eyes and see if you can actually feel what is stopping you from opening your turnout further. Is it the front of your hips (TFL?), inside your hip (Iliacus or Psoas Major?), inside the thighs (Adductors and Pectinous?), the sides of the hips (Gluteus Medius and Minimus?), the back of your hip (Hip Capsule or Sacroiliac Joint?), or even in your low back (Lumbosacral Joint - the junction where the lumbar vertebra of your spine unites with the sacrum). Check anatomical diagrams to identify possible structures which may be blocking your turnout. If you have access to a Physiotherapist or Doctor who works with dancers, they should be able to assess your hips to find where the blockage is located.

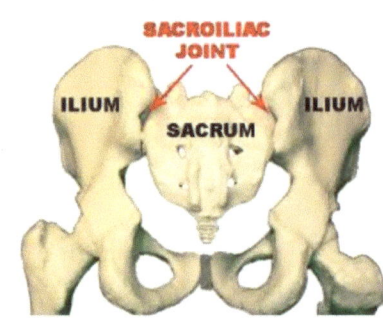

**Yoga Sitting Position**
*Helps restriction in the piriformis area. It is great for dancers who have a hard time holding turnout devant.*

**Fire Log**
*Helps restriction in the sides of the hips and stretches your gluteus medius.*

## RELEASE THESE POINTS OF RESTRICTION!

After finding your restriction, work only on releasing that area, not on turnout. When this area releases, it will allow you more turnout.

Each of the areas above have several ways to deal with restriction. The yoga sitting position and fire log are two yoga positions which will help turnout a lot.

**NOTE: Do not do these if you feel any pain.**

# FIND OUT WHY YOUR MUSCLES ARE TIGHT

The main step in resolving hip restriction is to find where the tension is coming from. Tension is being held by your body for a reason, and the true 'cure' for improving your range is to identify why those restricting muscles are tight in the first place. Your body is always adjusting and readjusting to the messages you give it. If you repeatedly tense up a muscle, it can continue holding that tension long after it's released. This happens for many reasons, but most often it is due to chronic emotional stress, anxiety, trying too hard, compensating for weaknesses elsewhere or faulty technique, just to name a few. Overworked muscles go into a constant state of contraction trying to perform their job. They eventually become exhausted and this limits what they can do.

Pay close attention to muscles that feel tense and practice relaxing them. For example: A lot of us hold the muscles of our lower neck and shoulders tense when we're working on the computer or studying. When we rub them, they feel sore from stored tension.

## Causes of Muscle Tension in Specific Areas

### Adductors (Inner Thighs)
- Constantly crossing legs when sitting.
- Overtraining one muscle - usually inner thigh range strength.
- Weakness of the stabilizers on the outside of the hip (Gluteus Medius).
- Weak pelvic floor (Causes adductors to grip in an attempt to stabilize the pelvis).

### Gluteus Medius and Minimus (Side of Hip)
- Gripping with all gluteals to hold turnout.
- Reduced isolation of true turnout muscles (Deep External Rotators).
- 'Sitting' in the hip.
- Overtraining of Gluteus Medius in shortened or non-functional positions.

### Rectus Femoris - A quadriceps muscles (front of thigh) and the TFL (front/side of hip)
- Overuse due to weakness of deeper hip flexors (psoas major and iliacus).
- Poor multifidus control (Deep Back Stabilizers).
- Reduced Pelvic Floor and Deep Abdominal control.
- Weakness in Oblique Abdominals.
- Hitching (lifting) the hip in retiré and développé à la seconde.

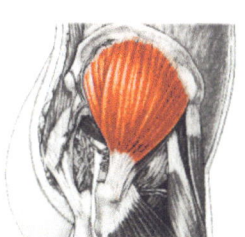

*Gluteus Medius for lifting your leg away from center, rotates the thigh when sitting or in retiré, and hip stabilization.*

# Factors for Creating a Great Extension w/ **EXCELLENT TURNOUT**

Achieving a beautiful, well-controlled développé by focusing only on flexibility or shear strength is not effective. You must be able to use your whole body from head to toe.

- Head and Neck = Face and jaw muscles for softness and strength.
- Back stabilization muscles = Torso control and mobility.
- Arms = Strong yet soft and fluid.
- Core = Strong with activated Iliopsoas muscles.
- Inner thigh = Strong use of adductors and sartorius.
- Legs = Enough range of flexibility and the strength to control that range.
- Knees = Adequate strength, control and lift to be held in neutral.
- Standing foot = Adequate strength, control and lift to hold your tripod stand and maintain center over the balancing points of your foot.

The psoas major is the main controller of height in your extension. This is why it is so important to develop strong stability muscles in your core and back as it frees the psoas from being used to stabilize your spine and allows it to be a more effective as a hip flexor in lifting your leg.

Not having strong stability muscles causes overuse of the TFL and rectus femoris. This can be felt as a gripping feeling in the top of your hip when doing a développé devant because the psoas major is busy controlling your spine, and the front of your leg has taken over your extension. See Waiter's Bow, Floor Développés and 4-Point Psoas (for holding your extension) exercises in Core and Back chapter.

# THE CLAM SERIES

**Purpose:** To strengthen the piriformis and other turnout muscles in the back of your hip.

## Technique

- While lying on the floor extend your lower arm and place your upper arm on your hip. Keep your waist up off the floor.

- Hold hips stacked and don't allow the top hip to pull back.

- Inhale while lifting, exhale and inhale while holding. Exhale while lowering.

- Check your hips often to make sure they remain stacked.

- Do piriformis stretches after these exercises to release tension in this area.

**The Clam:** Lie on your side with your knees bent to 90° and your knees, feet and hips stacked on top of each other of each other. Hinge your knee upward about 12" not allowing any movement in your hip. Hold 10 counts and return. Do 10x.

**Crazy Clam:** Lift your knee, hinging from your toes as above but as you lower your knee to the other knee, lift your foot. Hold 10 counts then lower your foot and raise your knee. Continue to alternate. Do 10x.

**Planked Clam:** As above, but resting on elbow and holding body straight from shoulder to knee.

# MORE **TURNOUT** STRENGTHENING EXERCISES

**Because the platform of a pointe shoe is so small, it's impossible to turnout by twisting your feet on the floor. Instead, you must use the strength of your turnout muscles.**

**Turnout Isolation:** Lie on stomach with legs parallel. Lift legs slightly off the floor keeping your back relaxed. Flex your feet. Turn legs out. Then point your toes maintaining turnout. Return your legs to parallel, and lower to starting position. Do 10x.

**Turnout in Retiré w/Theraband:** Stand facing the barre with theraband wrapped around thigh in retiré and barre. Maintaining hip squareness turnout knee further. Hold 10 counts and release. Do 5x.

**Wall Press:** Isometric strengthening exercise for the gluteus medius. Use these muscles to keep the hips level when standing on one leg. Stand w/side against wall and hands crossed on shoulders. Bend knees slightly, lift wall foot up in back to knee height keeping knees in line. Press knee to wall. Hold 8 seconds (keep hips level and deep core muscles working). Feel on outer hip. Repeat 3x.

**Piriformis Lift:** On hands and knees holding back in neutral throughout the exercise. Slowly rotate one knee outward maintaining its 90° angle and keeping hips square. Hold 10 counts and return.

**Frog:** Lay prone on the floor with your knees bent and out to the side. Hold your feet together with toes up and heels pressed down toward the floor as low as possible. Hold and relax. Having someone press you lower is not a good idea because it could force the ligaments and tendons beyond their capacity causing pain in your hips.

**Advanced Frog:** Now press up placing your forearms on the floor as in doing the cobra. Hold 10 counts and return. Move slowly and gently.

**Rond de Jambes:** Rond de Jambes are designed for turnout. Make sure you engage all your turnout muscles while doing them in class. Feel them working. This means both legs, not just the working leg. Your supporting leg turnout muscles must be equally engaged.

# STRETCHES FOR HIPS and TURNOUT

## PIRIFORMIS STRETCHES

**Purpose:** To release tension and increase flexibility in the piriformis and hip areas. Releasing tension in this area can help with splits. Do after all turnout exercises. Hold each stretch at least 30 counts.

**Lying Piriformis Stretch:** Lie on back with one leg straight, the other bent to 45° and raised. Without lifting the hip, hold ankle with opposite hand and place your toe in one hand and press your knee outward with the other, keeping knee directly in front of nose.

**Seated Piriformis Stretch:** Sit in a chair with the ankle of one leg on the knee of the other. Press your knee down. Maintaining a straight back, slowly press forward. Be sure back is straight and shoulders stay square.

**Seated Piriformis Stretch w/Twist:** Sit on floor with L leg straight and R bent over L. Press L elbow on outside of R knee, reach back with right arm and look back. Maintaining a straight back, slowly press forward. Hold when you feel a comfortable stretch in your hips and gluteals.

## ADDUCTOR STRETCHES

**Long Adductors:** Lie on your back with your bottom against a wall and your legs up the wall. Open your legs sideways as far as possible. Slowly turn your legs out and in. Hold 5 counts. Lift slightly and lower down a little further.

**Short Adductors:** As above with bottom about 8 to 10 inches from wall. Place feet on the wall 6 inches from floor with knees bent and lowered to side. (Hips should be even with knees.) Hold moving knees up and down a little.

**Standard Barre Stretch:** Face the barre and place one leg on the barre in 2nd. Keeping your hips and shoulders centered, slide as far across the barre as possible and return.

## TENSOR FASCIA LATE AND GLUTEAL STRETCHES

**Purpose:** The IT band is like a long piece of leather-like fascia that doesn't stretch and attaches to several hip muscles including the TFL, gluteus maximus and medius, keeping your hips aligned.

1. Lie on back with knees bent. Place one ankle on top of the other knee in turnout. Pull your ankle toward you and press the knee away. Hold.

2. Seated with legs straight in front. Bend one knee placing the foot on the floor across the other leg as shown in picture to right. Keep both hips on the floor. Press the bent knee toward the opposite side. Hold 10 counts, release and repeat.

3. Stand facing the barre. Place one leg on the barre bent to 90° with your knee and lower leg resting on the barre directly in front of you squarely in front of your hips. Hold 10 to 20 counts, release and repeat.

**Gluteal Stretches Continued:** Hold at least 30 counts.

*Lying Gluteal Stretch*

*Seated Gluteal Stretch*

# ILIOPSOAS SERIES

The iliacus and the psoas major and minor muscles combine to form a powerful hip flexor for your thigh which dancers use in extension. They attach from the lower vertebrae in your spine to your femur bone.

Think about this: If your core stability muscles (discussed in the next chapter) aren't strong enough to hold your alignment, your body will automatically start using the iliopsoas to stabilize your spine. As discussed before, it then won't be available for extension work. Then other weaker muscles will be called on for your extensions and will suffer from overuse. It's a house of cards. Building up your core stability muscles will free the iliopsoas for the job it does best—hip flection and your extension will really improve.

## Iliopsoas Strengthening

**Purpose:** The muscles of the iliopsoas are one of the main sets of muscles used in grand battement and développé extension.

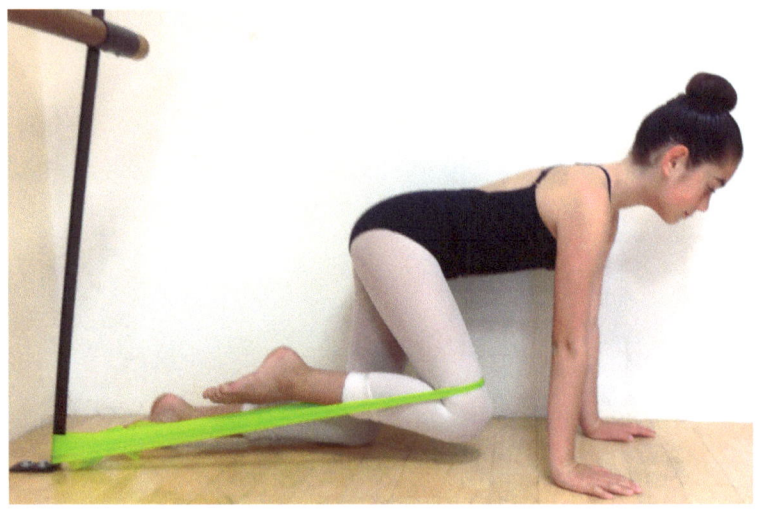

### Technique

1. Keep your spine in neutral and maintain placement.
2. Keep hands beneath your shoulders and knees below hips.
3. Stay relaxed in the outer hip and don't hitch up or tuck under.

**See extension exercises in Chapter 3.** They are primarily for strengthening the iliopsoas.

## Iliopsoas Stretching

**Purpose:** Stretching these muscles can increase the height of your arabesque extension derrière and make balancing easier.

**Seated Stretch:** Sit right hip on chair with right foot on floor with bent knee, hands on right thigh, leg in deep parallel lunge with heel up and knee straight. Press forward with left hip.

**Forward Lunge:** Be sure to keep your back up and press froward in your left hip for a good stretch in your iliopsoas (Note: Keep your foot straight below your knee unlike example #1 below).

The Deep Lunge    Kneeling Lunge (You can also bend your lower leg upward)

The Scorpion

**The Tired Dancer Stretch:** Lay face up on your bed. Place the top of your outside foot on the floor and slide it back, stretching your iliopsoas.

**The Tired Dancer Stretch #2:** Lay prone with one leg on and one off the bed in a forward lunge. Place hands under your shoulders and press up.

The Side Plank (shown in "Core and Back" chapter) is also a good multi-joint exercise which challenges the iliopsoas.

**Advanced Kneeling Lunge:** Place your back knee on floor and front foot on a step or bench. Lunge forward as far as possible keeping your heel beneath your knee.

Twist, placing your opposite elbow outside the front leg. Reach right arm back and bend your knee raising foot.

1. Be sure your hips remains square.
2. Be sure your heel remains directly below your knee.

The Deep Twisting Lunge

# ASSESSMENTS #15 - #22

## #15 and #16 - Degagés from 5th - 4x en Croix

**Purpose:** Demonstrating the ability to isolate your moving leg from your non-moving body, foot articulation, and maintain alignment.

**Errors:** Moving body, or tilting torso, unable to articulate or maintain turnout, clenched or clawed toes.

**Correction:** A placement/alignment issue: Keep your weight centered over standing leg (60/40) and maintain this alignment. Articulation not used.

## #17 and #18 - Single Leg Stand in Turnout

**Purpose:** To demonstrate foot, ankle, and lower leg control when balancing on one leg in demi-plié.

**Errors:** Tendons on the top and side of foot and ankle flick off and on, foot wobbles, toes claw or clench in an attempt to grab the floor. Turnout not held.

**Correction:** A strength issue. Muscles under the foot are not strong enough to hold your instep in place. Flicking tendons are your attempt to keep your instep steady from the top of your foot through the lower leg muscles. Strengthen the foot muscles.

## #19 and #20 - Single Leg Elevé in Parallel

**Purpose:** To demonstrate foot strength, as well as hip, core and back control in your ability to smoothly elevé in a parallel retiré to full demi-pointe without wobbling, balance for 3 counts and return with control.

**Errors:** Rolling off balancing point between big toe and 2nd toe, lifting hip, tilting torso to side or pulling shoulders back, clawing or clenching toes, wobbling ankles.

**Correction:** A strength and/or placement issue: Work on strengthening core, feet, and ankles as well as work on alignment.

## #21 and #22 - Single Leg Elevé in Turnout

**Purpose:** To demonstrate your ability to smoothly rise to full demi-pointe maintaining both legs in turnout. Balance for 3 counts and lower smoothly.

**Errors:** Losing turnout, balance and/or alignment, not reaching full demi-pointe height, clenching or clawing.

**Correction:** A strength and/or placement issue: Work on strengthening core, foot, ankle and turnout muscles along with alignment.

# ASSESSMENTS
# #15 - #22

| ASSESSMENTS | REQUIREMENTS TO PASS |
|---|---|
| **#15 and #16 - Degagé from 5th en Croix** | From 5th, do 4 slow, articulated degagés maintaining control and turnout. To improve torso control, keep weight distributed 60% on the ball of the foot and hold hips and shoulders squarely over these points. |
| **#17 and #18 - Single Leg Stand in Turnout** | From 1st, lift one foot to sur le cou-de-pied maintaining turnout, keeping weight 60% on the ball of the foot and hold with no movement for 10 counts. Flicking tendons are your body's attempt to maintain balance from the top of your foot. Learn to use the muscles within your foot to hold your balance. |
| **#19 and #20 - Single Leg Elevé in Parallel** | From a single leg stand, elevé into full demi-pointe with back held strongly and weight held between big toe and 2nd toe. Hold torso aligned with arms in 2nd. Balance 3 counts, and lower with control. Do not wobble, sickle, or flair the foot on elevé. |
| **#21 and #22 - Single Leg Elevé in Turnout** | From in 1st—arms in 2nd, slowly lift one foot to sur le cou-de-pied maintaining proper alignment. Elevé, slowly shifting your axis above your point of balance. Rise to full demi-pointe without lifting your hip or tilting your body. Hold 3 counts, and lower with control. Wobbling or losing your balance indicates lack of foot, ankle, and lower leg strength as well as balancing skills. |

# HIP PAIN

The hip joint, largest of our body's ball and socket joints, is surrounded by tendons, ligaments and cartilage/labrum which help to stabilize the ball within the socket.

## Hip Strains and Injuries

The illiofemeral ligament is a Y-shaped group of ligaments in front of the hips holding the femur to the pelvis. It can be strained when violently moved or jerked as in stretching at the barre, or with too many développés in 2nd before warming up sufficiently. This can also cause pain in the inside of the thigh. The height of your grand battement should be held down until you have developed sufficient strength, and your turnout is under control.

## Labral Tear

The labrum is a cup-like rim of fibrocartilage that surrounds the socket of the hip creating a suction-like effect holding, along with ligaments, the ball in the socket. A tear can occur in the lip of the fibrocartilage.

Though not common, a loose piece of cartilage from the tear can cause pain.

**Causes of a Labral Tear**

1. Degeneration - extremely flexible joints are at greater risk from repetitive use.
2. A sudden fall, twist, or blow.

**Symptoms of a Labral Tear are similar to other hip pain and can only be diagnosed by your doctor.**

1. Snapping or clicking in the hip.
2. A sharp catching pain.
3. A deep groin pain.
4. An unstable feeling in the hip.
5. Pain that worsens when flexing or rotating the hip.
6. A limited range of motion.
7. Discomfort laying on the injured side.

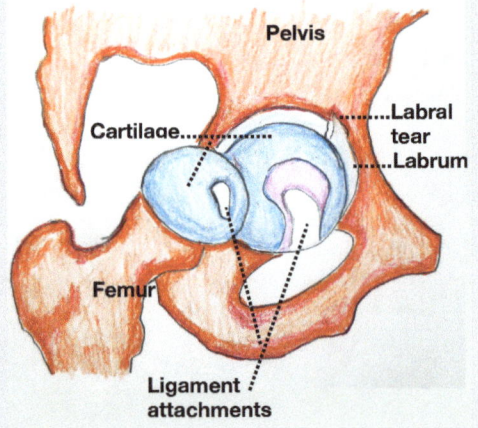

**Treatment**

1. Apply a cold compress to the area to control pain and swelling.
2. Modify or limit activity.
3. Ultrasound has been mentioned.
4. See your doctor.

## Piriformis Syndrome

The piriformis lies directly over the sciatic nerve as it travels down the leg. Because of this, a disorder called "Piriformis Syndrome" can occur if the sciatic nerve is pressed or irritated by the piriformis. This can casue pain, tingling and numbness in the buttock which runs along the path of sciatic nerve and down into the leg. If you're gripping too much with your turnout muscles in class, you may experience this condition.

Turnout muscles are designed to activate and release, however, sometimes dancers can try a little too hard! Gripping with the gluteals and/or turnout muscles can result in excessive tension in the piriformis muscle. This tension then causes pressure on the sciatic nerve as it passes through or beneath it.

## Sciatica

A set of symptoms including pain that may be caused by pressing on and/or iirritating the sciatic nerve. Sciatica pain is felt in the lower back and can radiate down the leg. It is relatively common. If you do have piriformis syndrome, however, focus on stretching and releasing tension in the piriformis area and learn to not grip in the hip so much when you dance.

## The Unlocked Sacroiliac Joint

When we stand on one leg normally, this joint goes through a small amount of rotation which locks it into place allowing us to balance on this leg without excessive muscular force. This is called "Form Closure." If the SI Joint does not lock in place, the muscles that cross this joint (namely, you guessed it - the piriformis) have to forcibly contract to stabilize it, called "Force Closure." If the piriformis is constantly contracting to stabilize the pelvis, and you are turning as well, the piriformis will become very overworked and tight. This can also happen with hypermobile dancers.

## Check for Gluteal Firing

If your gluteals are not working properly then the hamstrings may start taking on too much of the load when you are walking or dancing. Inactive gluteal muscles, (as when one sits all day long) also adds to the development of piriformis syndrome. Rolling ankles and knees can also cause an excessive load on the piriformis.

If any of these issues are a problem for you, consult an Osteopath or Physiotherapist who works with pelvic mechanics. The adjustments needed can be very minor and can make a BIG difference in how stable you are through the pelvis.

The piriformis lies directly over the sciatic nerve as it travels down the leg.

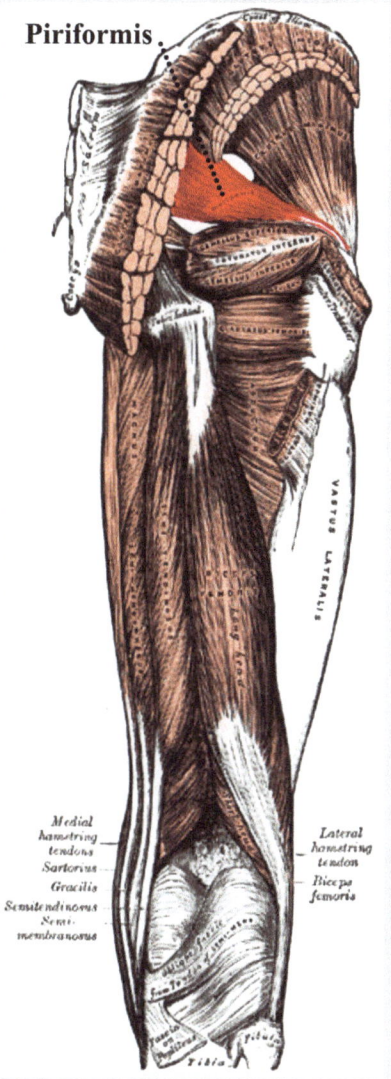

# Chapter 5
## ASSESSMENTS 23 - 28

# Core and Back

A vital part of pointe work is core control. To relevé on a single leg is impossible without it.

# SUMMARY
## Chapter 5
# CORE AND BACK

Core control is vital to back control. It is essential in maintaining our posture, holding our balance, managing correct back arches, and performing successful pirouettes.

Our core and back have two types of muscle groups — movement or fast-twitch muscles and posture or slow-twitch muscles.

## MOVEMENT MUSCLES:

Outer muscles, which move us in all directions, are mainly made of fast twitch cells which burn energy quickly and tire rather soon.

### Making Them Stronger

These muscles made stronger through lots of repetitions.

### Making Them Longer

Besides being strong, movement muscles must be stretched to release tension as well as create and sustain flexibility.

## POSTURE MUSCLES:

These muscles are located deep inside our bodies close to our bones and act to hold these bones in place. Their cells are mainly slow twitch, burning energy slowly with a staying power that lasts a long time.

### Making Them Stronger

These are muscles are made stronger through a sustained hold with very little movement.

### What Happens If They Aren't Strong Enough?

If these muscles don't have the strength to complete their job, movement muscles take over. The problem is that movement muscles then won't be available for their task and will also tire quickly.

## MUSCLES OF THE CORE

## STABILITY MUSCLES

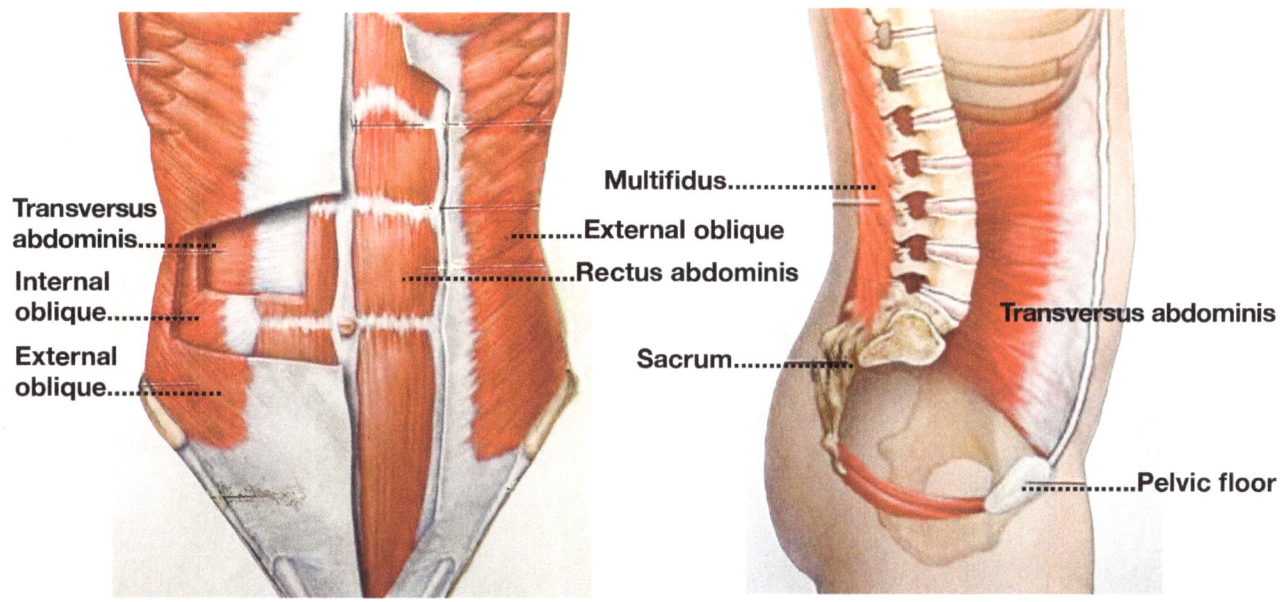

1. **Rectus Abdominis:** The outside core muscles (6 pack) = Strengthened by doing sit ups and crunches. It bends the body forward.

2. **External Obliques:** Superficial muscles angle downward. They pull the trunk downward and aid somewhat in twisting and side-bends.

3. **Internal Obliques:** Lying below the external obliques, these muscles angle upward. They oppose the diaphragm in breathing out and rotates and bends the trunk to the side.

4. **Transversus Abdominis:** The deepest layer of muscle, which wraps from the spine around the side and joins fascia in the abdomen. When contracted, it narrows the waist. It supports the abdominal wall, helps in breathing out, and helps stabilize the spine.

1. **Multifidus:** Very thin muscles that lie deep inside the back and fill the groove on each side of the spine running from the sacrum to the shoulder area attaching to every vertebra and stabilizing each segment of the spine.

2. **Transversus Abdominis:** They help to compress the ribs and stabilize the spine, pelvis, and thorax. It's a challenge to learn to activate these muscles without engaging your oblique muscles. Exercise: Lay on your back, placing your fingers on the outside of your hip bones and your thumbs pressing inside. When you contract this muscle, your thumbs will feel it. It doesn't take much of a contraction. If you contract more, you will engage the obliques.

# MUSCLES OF THE BACK SHOULDERS

1. **The trapezius** are large surface muscles of the back. They lift, rotate, and inwardly pull the scapulas and shoulders.

2. **Rhomboids major and minor** lay under the trapezius and rotate as well as inwardly pull the scapulas (shoulder blade).

3. **Latissimus dorsi** pull the shoulders down and back. They also help pull the scapula downward.

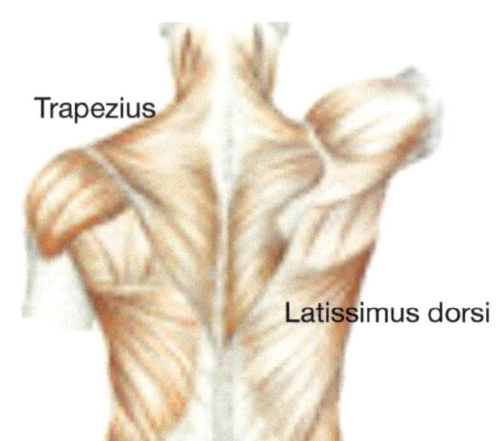

**Superficial muscles of the back are are for movement & not wanted for stabilizing the spine.**

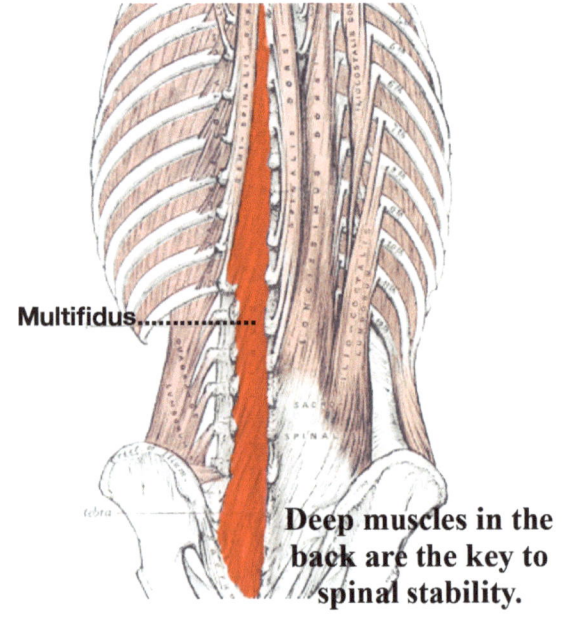

**Deep muscles in the back are the key to spinal stability.**

**Multifidus**
These muscles are among the smallest in our body, yet they are extremely powerful and work together with the transverse abdominous and pelvic floor to stabalize the spine (slow twitch). This stabilization must happen before arm and leg movement can take place. They also take pressure off the discs separating each vertabrae. Their strength is essential to good back health.

**Erector Spinae (Shown to right of spine.)**
A very long group of muscles in the back which work to straighten, arch, rotate and bend the back. When you allow your shoulders to slump forward and chest to sink downward, these muscles are not working.

# ABOUT THE CORE AND BACK

## Back and Core Muscles

1. **Movement Muscles** (fast-twitch) are designed to move your torso taking strong, quick action in movements like bending, lifing, or pulling. Their strength, however, doesn't last.

2. **Posture Muscles** (slow-twitch) are designed to hold your spine upright for long periods of time.

When your back gets tired and aches from standing or sitting for a long time, the deep muscles within your torso—the multifidus in your back, transversus abdominis in your core and your pelvic floor—have stopped working correctly. Now the larger outer muscles must step in so your back can remain stabilized. Unfortunately, these big back muscles—erector spinae, lattissimus dorsi, etc—tire quickly, and your back becomes stiff and sore, making you feel like you need to move around, stretch out, or crack your back.

## Core stability is essential to master before going on pointe!

**If you are unable to hold your torso in alignment, you will never be able to stand on one leg en pointe.** Every dance technique requires intense torso control, which is provided by core and back strength. Your spine must be held strong throughout all combinations so your legs can move freely with both control and speed. Leaps, jumps, and turns are impossible without outstanding torso control. Jacque Haas of Human Kinetics tells us there are studies which show a grand jeté can create a landing force of up to 12 times your body weight. Your ability to control these landings is key in preventing injury. This is why it is so important to have great core and back strength, as well as excellent use of your instep and plié with each landing.

Exercises on the following pages range from the most basic to the very difficult and are for strengthening the inner most muscles of the core and back.

Besides the exercises for core strength and stability on the following pages, two very important ones to master are simply front and side leg lifts. As you practice all these exercises, make sure you do them properly and make the corrections given.

# STABILITY STRENGTHENING Series

**Purpose:** To create strong, reliable stability muscles which hold the spine.

**The Basic Vacuum:** Lie on the floor on your back with legs stretched. Place one hand below your back and the other on your tummy. Draw your bellybutton inward and upward not allowing your back to push against your hand. Hold 20 counts breathing normally. Relax and repeat.

**NOTE: INCLUDE THIS TECHNIQUE THROUGHOUT THE FOLLOWING EXERCISES.**

**Standing Vacuum:** Repeat the basic vacuum, standing. Be sure to press inward and maintain a neutral posture without moving your spine.

**The Waiter's Bow:** Repeat the standing vacuum and, while pressing inward, bend forward from your hips to 20°. Hold 20 counts, and return. Be sure your back stays straight. Repeat this bow to 45°. Then repeat as far as you can with a straight back. It is interesting to note that should you be able lock one leg and straighten up with it at this angle - voila! There is your extension.

**Floor Développés:** Lie on the floor with legs straight and feet on a wall 6 inches off the floor in 1st position. Place hands as in the basic vacuum drawing your bellybutton in and hold, breathing normally. In turnout, bring one foot to retiré and développé to the ceiling. Hold, not allowing your back to push down to your hand. Lower the leg to the wall in 1st and repeat with the other leg.

## *Technique*

1. Maintain back in neutral, not allowing it to press down on your hand as it prevents the small stability muscles on the back of your spine from working.

2. Pull in and up through your lower abdomen engaging your core stability muscles.

3. For Bug Legs, breathe out when you extend your leg and while bringing your leg in.

4. There should no pain in your back.

5. Keep your movements slow and deliberate.

###  BUG LEGS:

Lye with legs bent and held at 90 degrees.   Stretch one leg out at 45 degrees and return.

# PLANK Series

**Purpose:** To increase core and spine control, strength and stability, providing our bodies with effortless strength and fluidity in the trunk through isometric contraction. Planks are wonderfully versatile exercises. You can begin at the most basic and work up. Planks are rated as the top exercise for toning the abdominals. One side is usually less stable than the other, so do twice as many on your weaker side.

Modified Planks

Basic Plank

Beginning Side Plank

Advanced Plank

Knee Plank

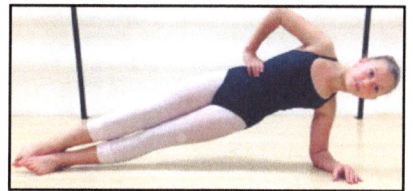
Intermediate Side Plank

### Technique

1. Keep hips in line with feet and shoulders throughout.

2. Don't allow your head to drop. Keep it in line with the rest your body.

3. Hold strong without wobbling for 20 counts. Rest 3 counts and repeat.

4. One side is usually less stable that the other. Do 2x as often on your weaker side.

Plank and Pike

127

# BACK STRENGTHENING Series

**Purpose:** A well-conditioned back can withstand more stress, bear more weight, and better protect your spine from injury.

**Intermediate Plank**

**Advanced Plank**

**Cobra Twist**

> ### Technique
>
> **PLANK**
>
> 1. Maintain a straight plank hold throughout exercise.
> 2. Raise arm without twisting shoulder.
>
> **COBRA TWIST**
>
> 3. Hold shoulders down and open with neck long showing no tension.
> 4. Hold legs together.
> 5. You may have a helper hold your feet or place them under a low chair.
>
> **YOGA CAT: BACK WAVE**
>
> *Keep spine in slow continuous rolling motion, moving one vertebra at a time.*

Raise back and arms up while breathing in. Twist right breathing out. Return to center breathing in and repeat L. Breath out lowering to floor. Rest for 2 breaths and repeat twisting left first. Do 6 sets.

### The Yoga Cat: With Continuous Roll

On hands and knees, tilt your tailbone under (shown on next page). Slowly press each vertebra one at a time upward until your shoulders and neck are rounded upward and your head is down. Then slowly tilt your tail bone upward, followed by each vertebra pressing down until the upper back, shoulders and neck are lowered, and your head is up. Keep the roll moving slow and even. Do 10x.

# BACK STRETCHING Series

**Purpose:** Stretching these muscles keeps your back flexible and helps in preventing pain and injury.

**The Yoga Cat Stretch:** For strengthening the multifidus. Change with each breath.

**The Yoga Cat With Continuous Roll:** On hands and knees, tilt your tail bone under (as shown above). Slowly press each vertebra one at a time upward until your shoulders and neck are rounded upward and your head is down. Then slowly tilt your tail bone upward, followed by each vertebra pressing down until the upper back, shoulders, and neck are lowered and your head is up. Keep the roll moving slow and even. Do 10x.

### Erector Spinae Exercises:

Engage your core and breathe in, arching your back as in picture on left. Then round forward. Similar to the Cat Stretch.

NOTE: Keep your neck stretched and head from dropping down in back. Breathe out as you contract forward through your core, moving shoulders forward. Round your spine as far as possible. Repeat 5x.

*Triangle Stretch*  *The Cobra*  *Twisting Lunge*

# ASSESSMENTS 23 - 28

## #23 and #24 - Advanced Plank

**Purpose:** To demonstrate torso stability and strength on both sides.
**Errors:** Bottom up, wobbling, twisting, arm and/or leg too low.
**Correction:** A stability issue. Deep core and back stability muscles lack the strength and endurance to maintain this position. Do core stability exercises from this chapter.

## #25 and #26 - Single Leg Sauté

**Purpose:** To demonstrate foot, ankle, and lower leg strength as well as torso stability.
**Errors:** Hip of the raised foot lifts during sauté, heavy or rolled landing, hip of the raised foot drops during landing.
**Correction:** A foot, ankle, and leg strength issue. Muscles of your foot, ankle and calf lack the strength to lift your body off the floor. Trying to lift with your hip.

## #27 and #28 - Superman with a Twist

**Purpose:** To demonstrate back strength and stability.
**Errors:** Unable to complete 10 times in one continuous combination.
**Correction:** A strength issue in your back. Do back and shoulder exercises several times a day to increase strength.

## Working More Effectively in Class:

- Stretch up through your back with ribs in and body aligned.
- Use your feet fully pushing strongly away from the floor with each jump, and always roll your landings well with toe, ball, heel, plié into a tripod stand.
- With the first breath of each movement, engage your core.

# ASSESSMENTS #23 - #28

| ASSESSMENTS | REQUIREMENTS TO PASS |
|---|---|
| **#23 and #24 - Advanced Plank** | Lay prone with hands below your shoulders and toes on the floor. Press up to the plank position. Stretch your left arm forward and lift your right leg. Hold for 10 counts. Return to starting position with control. |
| **#25 and #26 - Single Leg Sauté** | Stand in 5th and demi-plié lifting one foot to sur le cou de pied. Sauté with a full point without lifting your hip, pulling through your back, or changing your posture. |
| **#27 and #28 - Superman with Twist** | Lay prone with arms over head. Slowly lift arms and chest off the floor and hold 5 counts. Twist right holding 5 counts, return to center holding 5 counts, twist left holding 5 counts. Return to center holding 5 counts. This is your first set. Do 5 sets. |

# SCOLIOSIS

Coming from a Greek word meaning crooked, scoliosis is a condition where the spine curves and/or twists abnormally. The estimation is that it affects 4 1/2% of the population and is twice as common in girls.

## The Symptoms and Signs of Scoliosis

An abnormal curve in the spine may slowly become noticeable. Clothes may not fit quite right or pant legs may be longer on one side than the other. It may cause the head to appear off center, one hip or shoulder to be higher than the other, or the ribs on one side to curve further out than the other.

If this condition is a concern, the first thing to do is get a correct diagnosis and evaluation by your doctor. Treatment is based on the severity and type of each case and can consist of observation, education, specific exercises, bracing and for a final solution — surgery.

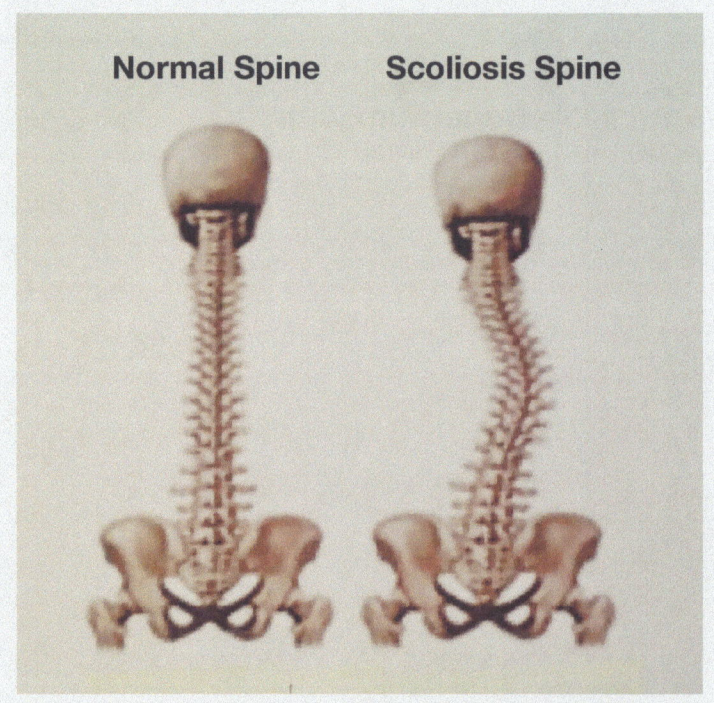

Exercise treatments for scoliosis are evolving, and there is some evidence for the benefit, but various exercise methods are not known by the scientific community nor have enough scientific studies been conducted to confirm their theories.

No one knows what causes the most common type of scoliosis called idiopathic (say: ih-dee-uh-pa-thik) scoliosis. (Idiopathic is a fancy word for unknown cause.) Doctors do know that scoliosis can run in families.

# SCOLIOSIS Exercises

**Purpose:** Exercise will strengthen and stretch the muscles of the back and shoulder area. Be sure to consult your doctor when considering an exercise course for scoliosis.

There are many who believe that scoliosis can be better treated through exercise. The Scoliosis Rehabilitation Center states that "bracing NEVER reduces the curvature, and surgery is only temporary" and believe in a non-bracing, non-surgical alternative treatment. They also state that the standard treatment is to wait and see, checking with x-rays periodically. Should the curvature reach 25 degrees a hard brace can be prescribed. If progress continues, then surgery is recommended.

Below are exercises which have been recommended by others to help strengthen and stretch the back. Their effect on Scoliosis is unknown.

### Exercises for strengthening and stretching the back, which have previously been covered:

- All Core Stability Exercises.
- Superman (can be done on stability ball with toes on floor).
- Core and Back Stretches.
- Exercises in "Back and Shoulder Blade Series" (chapter 1).

### New Exercises:

- **Triceps Raise:** Seated on a chair or stability ball. Hold a weight in your right hand and lift straight over head with your other hand holding the front of your elbow. Maintain a straight back with square lowered shoulders. Lower the weight behind you keeping your elbow up and return slowly, 10x repeat, 3 sets on each side.
- **Exercise for a spine curving to the side:** Standing with the outward curve of your spine toward a wall. Step into a forward parallel lunge with the wall foot forward. Maintaining your hips squarely, reach your outside arm over your head and place it on the wall. Without twisting your shoulders, reach your other arm across the front of your body toward the opposite wall. Hold 10 counts, release for 3 counts and repeat. Do 10x, repeating several times a day. Do side lifts to also strengthen the muscles which support the outwardly curving side.

**Consult your doctor before engaging in these exercises.**

# TIPS FOR AVOIDING BACK PAIN

✓ *Warm ups are important, so don't forget to warm up your back muscles too.*
✓ *Having a strong core helps support your back and aids in preventing injury.*

**NOTE:** Allowing your core to release and back to sway, places a lot of pressure in the small of your back and can cause it to ache. However, when your core is working and held strong, it lengthens your lower back relieving that pressure.

**Grand battement or développé derrière** can put strain on your lower back when taken in a full upright position, especially if your shoulder is pulling back. In this case, keep your back lifted but allow your pelvis to tilt forward a little.

**If, when arching back,** you allow your spine to bend only in the small of your back, you place the full weight of your upper body on just a few vertebrae in this area (see below). This places a great deal of strain in your lumbar discs which could lead to a rupture. Instead, pull up in your core to support the lower back, and don't allow your pelvis to shift forward or tilt. Keep your neck lengthened, and bend from the top of your shoulders one vertebra at a time down your spine. This way, your back bend is taken through your entire spine.

**Listen to your body.** Dancers need to learn what their body means when it sends out signals. An ache, or worse yet, a muscle spasm in the low back is telling you to stretch out, rest and/or examine your technique. Don't push into pain.

# BACK PAIN

Back pain is the most common complaint among American adults. There are many causes for back pain, but dancers need to be aware of only three.

**Injury**

**1. Spondylolisthesis or displaced disk:** When the disc slips out of position, usually at the base of the spine. This most commonly happens in gymnastics or active students. See a doctor.

**2. Herniated Lumbar Disk:** When the rubbery (in children, gel-filled) pad between two vertebra is injured and swells, pushing through its tough outer membrane. This protrusion can press on a nerve, causing a lot of pain.

**Mechanical Conditions**

**1. Spondylolysis:** One of the most common complaints in dancing. It is a type of stress fracture of the spine caused by repetitive bending. If a vertebra doesn't have enough strength and becomes overloaded, a stress fracture can occur. Note: This condition becomes more common if a dancer is not eating well. See a doctor.

**2. Fatigue:** When your back aches due to weakness from its supporting muscles.

**Acquired Conditions**

**1. Scoliosis:** Curvature of the spine, which we've covered before.

**2. Arthritis:** A general term, which consists of several types and causes, but generally it is a degenerating deformation of the bones due to overuse, injury, heredity, and/or age.

**Prevention:** WebMD recommends regular exercise, especially core and back work. Keep a healthy weight, wear good shoes, and don't smoke, as it ages the spine. Maintain good posture, whether standing or sitting.

Chapter 6

## ASSESSMENTS 29 - 36

## *Balance, Pirouette and Arabesque*

# SUMMARY
## Chapter 6
# BALANCE, PIROUETTE, ARABESQUE

When we move from two feet to one, then rise up in elevé or relevé and finally on to pointe, we continue demanding more from our balancing skills. To accomplish this rise, we must have extremely strong feet, ankles, lower leg and core muscles as well as fantastic centering and alignment skills.

## BALANCE:

Have you ever noticed you have good days and bad days? There are times when our bodies aren't working as well as we would like. Semicircular canals can also have off days, and they have a big influence on our balance.

## PIROUETTE:

Balancing while you turn requires aligning your body along its axis and holding it directly on your point of balance throughout the turn. Any small shift will cause you to fall out of the turn. Your head must spot around this axis, too. Your arms must be strong, yet not stiff, well-placed and move with ease and control.

## ARABESQUE:

In an arabesque, you'll extend different parts of your body equally away from the axis line in order to maintain balance. Keep your hips and shoulders square and aligned until you become advanced.

# Balance

*Not a trick or accident, but a matter of properly aligning your bones*

In our everyday lives, we constantly make adjustments in the balancing skills we've learned since we were babies learning to walk. In dance, just as when you were young, you keep making adjustments, fine tuning each movement until you can find center. With each challenge, you teach your brain how to balance.

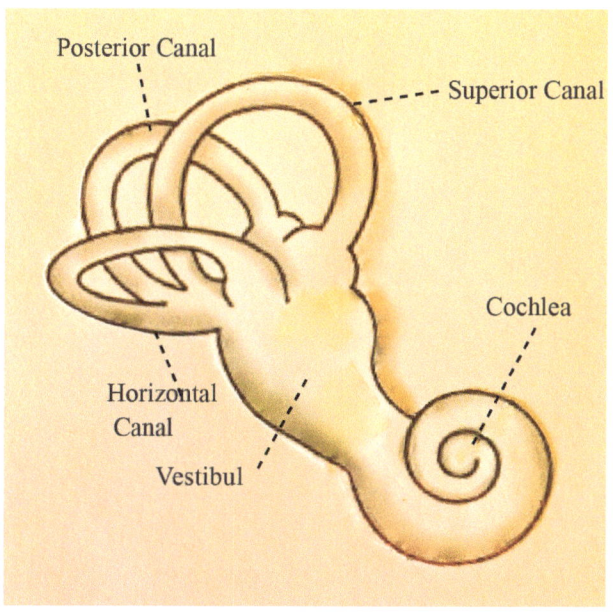

## THE SEMICIRCULAR CANALS

Without our semicircular canals, we couldn't even determine up from down let alone able to stand upright. These canals are the reason we become seasick as well as feel dizzy when turning. It's our brain responding to signals sent by our semicircular canals. In dance, we train our brains to become used to turning as well as through spotting, which helps orient us after each rotation.

Swelling or blockage around these canals (as with bad allergies), can throw our balance off by creating pressure.

**Our brains are geared for action, coordinating all parts of our body with each movement and issuing adjustments that will bring us into balance.**

### IMPROVE YOUR BALANCE BY CLOSING YOUR EYES

- Elevé in 1st, close your eyes and hold for 10 counts. Open your eyes and lower.
- With eyes closed elevé in 1st, tilt your head right, hold 5 counts, return to center and repeat left and lower.
- With eyes closed, elevé in 1st, raise your head, hold 5 counts, lower head, then lower to 1st.
- With eyes closed, elevé in 5th to full demi-pointe. Lower your heels slowly making yourself aware of all movements in your body. Repeat 10x.

# The Physics of **BALANCE**

## .Balance: Stability produced through the even distribution of weight on each side of a vertical axis.

### Axis:

A straight line through the center of the body around which that body rotates. For dancers, it's the line along which they find perfect alignment for balance and turning.

### Point of Balance:

In relevé the point where your foot contacts the floor, your axis extends, and your turn revolves.

### Pirouette Alignment:

The ability to maintain equal weight distribution along an axis vertical to your point of balance.

Axis

Point of Balance

### WHAT KEEPS A TURN GOING?

1. Spotting—keep your nose over your chin and eyes returning to the same place you left (slightly above eye level).

2. Maintaining alignment—hold your body as a well-placed unit, not separate parts.

3. Timing—moving each part of your body to the appropriate place at the correct moment.

# EXERCISES TO IMPROVE BALANCE

NOTE: These exercises have been shown in earlier chapters and should be revisited, if there are any questions.

NOTE: One side is often weaker than the other. Do twice as many on the weak side.

### A. Core Stability Series

**Purpose:** Improve core strength.

**Exercise:** See chapter 5.

### B. Demi-pointe Balance (Do Gastrocnemius and Soleus stretches when finished.)

**Purpose:** Finding center - keep weight slightly forward - lift out of center - use abdominals and turnout muscles to hold your position.

**Exercise:** Side to barre in 1st, place outside foot in retiré and elevé to demi-pointe. Slowly lift hand from barre, stretching out of the core. Balance 5 counts, retiré and lower. Do 5x.

### C. Rises with Theraband (Do Gastrocnemius and Soleus stretches when finished.)

**Purpose:** Increases foot and ankle control enormously.

**Exercise:** Loop theraband around your ankle and heel and a stationary object. Make theraband taunt and place feet in parallel with hands on hips. Slowly elevé and lower. Keep ankles aligned. Do 10x.

*NOTE: When this exercise is mastered: Repeat in 5th.*

### D. Eccentric Three Legged Cat (Do Piriformis Stretch after this exercise.)

**Purpose:** Hip and core control. Use of Gluteus Maximus.

**Exercise:** On hands and knees, extend one leg back. Lift leg until parallel to the floor. The important part of this exercise is in the eccentric phase (lowering of the leg). When lowering the leg, keep the pelvis perfectly still, core active, and make sure your spine at the shoulders doesn't sink downward. Keep back in neutral and motionless. Lower leg 4 counts, lift on 5th count. Ankle weights can be used for more resistance. Do 10x.

### E. Plank Series

**Purpose:** Core and back strength, control and stability.

**Exercise:** See exercises under core and back.

# CENTER FLOOR EXERCISES TO IMPROVE BALANCE

### A. Single Leg Stand - Hold each 10 sec

**Purpose:** To increase a dancer's balancing skills.

**Exercise:**

1. Stand in parallel on one leg with other foot sur la cou de pied.
2. Repeat with eyes closed.
3. Repeat inciting or turning the head from side to side.
4. Repeat above in turnout.

### B. Double Leg then Single Leg Elevé - Hold 3 seconds, repeating 3x

**Purpose:** Stabilize ankles and improve balance.

**Exercise:** Note: Pay close attention to prevent problems listed on the previous page. Use control when rising and lowering.

1. With feet in 6th position - elevé slowly and lower slowly.
2. Turnout in 1st – elevé maintaining your turnout.

### C. Relevé Passé From 5th

**Purpose:** Combines previous skills; to demonstrate coordination of body parts.

**Exercise:** Stand in 5th, relevé passé, hold, close 5th back. Do 10x 3x/day.

*(DO CALF STRETCHES AFTER THESE EXERCISES.)*

# How to Do a PIROUETTE

### Preparation

Whether beginning in 4th, 5th or a lunge, deeply demi-plié with well turned out knees over your toes. Be sure your hips are square, core is engaged, back is erect, shoulders are open and down, and your torso is aligned and stabilized.

Hold your arms strong yet not stiff with elbows lifted. The arm of your supporting foot is in 2nd and not allowed to twist behind your body. (This rotates the shoulders and pulls your body out of alignment.)

Establish your spot slightly higher than your eyes in relevé.

### Relevé Passé

PUSH straight up to relevé retiré, aligning the ball of your supporting foot directly beneath your correctly placed and centered body. Pull up on a well turned out stretched supporting leg. Keep the hips and shoulders square and keep your head erect, not raised or inclined.

The toes of your raised foot stay in contact with your knee without resting on the knee or sickling.

Before you begin turning, however, be sure you've developed your relevé skills and have the strength to hold and balance your relevé on full demi-pointe and can balance for at least 3 counts, returning with control.

### Turn

As you relevé, immediately press your working leg up to retiré, open your front arm strongly to 2nd (not thrown or opened behind your shoulder) quickly joined by your 2nd arm. Keep your shoulders down with elbows lifted. Head remains front but not too long before snapping erectly around returning to focus on the same focal point. Maintain center and body placement throughout each turn.

### Ending

Your pirouette ends UP on demi-pointe and in control. Spring down when you are ready, not because you are falling out of your pirouette.

# Perfecting PIROUETTES

*Pirouettes must be clean — extremly clean!*
*Reaching this level of excellence, however, requires fine tuning many, many skills.*

### YOUR PREPARATION

**Plié is more than bending your knees**, it's the launching pad for your turn.

**Make it solid:** Press down in your tripod stand with both feet.

**Make it well placed:** Be aware of each part of your body's placement: Keep your 4th narrow, turnout opened, shoulders square, one arm in 2nd, the other 5th front.

**Make it strong:** Give it the spring to place you directly over your point of balance.

### YOUR TAKEOFF

**As well as placing your axis straight above your balancing point, your takeoff establishes the torque and force you need for turning.**

**Make it fast:** Spring quickly to retiré. Most dancers fall out of their pirouette because their foot is too slow arriving at the knee.

**Make it straight:** Align your axis straight over your point of balance.

**Make it grounded:** Never allow your foot to hop up or lose contact with the floor.

**Make it strong:** Push off with both feet onto full demi-pointe.

### BALANCE AND ALIGNMENT

**Make it centered:** Unevenly distributed weight will cause you to fall out of your turn.

**Make it stretched:** Pull up through your body, engaging your core, and push down through the floor.

### ARMS AND HEAD

**Make them controlled.** Begin in a well-placed position and without twisting, open your arms with only the force needed to complete one turn. Snap the head erectly around, and return to the same spot.

### MULTIPLE TURNS

**Make them only after perfecting single turns:** First, master relevé on demi-pointe then quarter, half, and single turns. Only then is it time for multiple pirouettes.

**Don't rush multiple turns.**

# TRAINING YOUR HEAD

## Exercise:

Relevé in 5th with hands on shoulders and bourrée slowly turning in place. Spot your head, making sure it stays erect throughout your turn.

 **Don't set your spot too low. Keep it a little above eye level.**  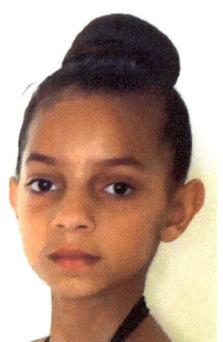 **Keep your head erect while spotting.**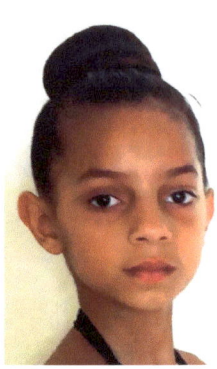

Select a spot a little above eye level, not too low. Hold your head erect with the chin directly below your nose.

Begin to spot before your chin reaches your shoulder. Waiting too long will force your head to incline.

**Don't raise, incline, or lower your head as you spot.**

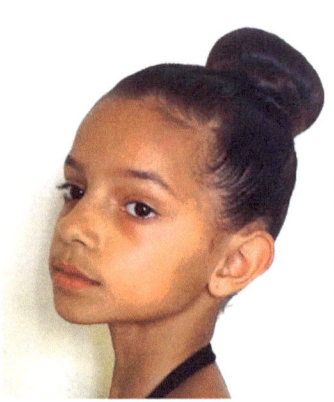  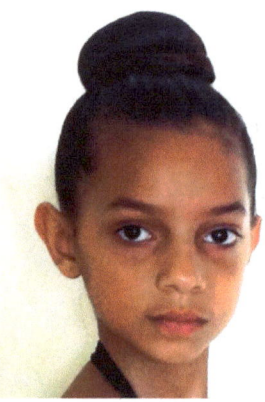

Hold your head erect throughout your entire spot. Don't allow it to raise, lower, incline or any combination of these. It simply makes a quick snap from one side to the other. Raising, inclining or lowering your head during a spot will give you lots of problems with pirouettes or turns across the floor by throwing you off your center.

# TRAINING YOUR ARMS

## Arm Placement When Turning

**Basic preparatory arm:** When in your preparatory position, the arm of your front foot is in à la seconde with the other held devant.

1. Press (do not throw) your front arm quickly to 2nd. *This indicates the direction of your turn.*
2. Quickly follow with the second arm pulling from 2nd to meet the first as you arrive at the back of your turn. *This is your power arm.*
3. As your turn reaches the 3/4 mark, leave the last arm there and complete your turn.

Arms are extremely important in pirouettes. They must be held strong yet not stiff, extended from the back, and lifted from beneath to provide needed stabilization to your turns.

**Correct**

**Correct**

Twisting or throwing your arms and upper body during a preparation throws off your alignment and negates the resistance needed for turning.

Both weak (as with dropped elbows) and tense arms hamper your ability to turn by giving your upper body either not enough, or too much resistance.

**Incorrect**

**Incorrect**

**Locating en Avant:** The proper placement of arms in front is located directly in front of the sternum. Place your fingers on the edge of your ribs. Walk them upward and inward until they meet. This is your sternum arch. Now stretch your arms forward. This is where your arms are placed en avant. Now press your core inward as if holding a large ball.

# TRAINING YOUR BODY

## Creating a Strong Foundation for Your Pirouettes

1. Continue increasing your foot, ankle and lower leg strength with exercises learned in Chapter Two. Do these exercises until you have developed the power to control a single leg elevé, balance without wobbling and return with control. Then progress to relevé.
2. The strength of your core and stability muscles are extremely important in pirouettes. Continue core and back stability training until you can balance in a single leg elevé/relevé (well centered and aligned), hold for 3 counts and end with control.

## Practice Balancing for Pirouettes

- **Balancing at the barre**: Stand in retiré—release barre and hold 10 counts.
  Elevé in 5th—release barre and hold 10 counts.
  Relevé on one leg—release barre and hold 3 counts.

- **Balancing center floor:** See if you can do these exercises center floor.

NOTE: Most dancers raise their hip slightly causing their upper body to tilt away from the raised leg (see page 23). Keep your hips square.

**Standing Passé**

**Relevé in 5th**

**Relevé Passé**

**Some day en Pointe**

### Work on:

- Engaging your core
- Lengthening your back
- Keeping weight forward on the foot's ball
- Maintaining square hips
- Opening both legs in turnout
- Holding shoulders down and open

**NOTE:** There are 2 ways to relevé. 1. (Cecchetti) Snatch the ball of your foot under your body's axis, or 2. (Vaganova) Move your body's axis over to the ball of your foot. Either way, your foot must never leave the floor.

# ABOUT YOUR PIROUETTES

## Points to Remember When Turning

1. Think of your pirouette as a relevé, not as a turn.
2. Both feet push off the floor from a strong, well turned out and centered plié.
3. Push up onto full demi-pointe with your body centered over the balancing point on the ball of your foot. Avoid rolling over onto your little toe.
4. Extend your arms outward from your shoulder blades as they press down and out, lifting from beneath your elbows.
5. Engage and stabilize your core and back muscles.
6. Keep hips and shoulders squarely centered over the ball's balancing point. Do not lift your hip.
7. Continue turning through spotting and remaining balanced on your rotational axis.
8. Attack your pirouettes, don't creep into them. Be confident with each strong relevé.
9. End your turn because you choose to, not because you have to.
10. Remain aware of the center line running up from the floor through the top of your head.
11. Spot with your head erect, returning to the same spot with each turn.

## Problems with Falling Out of Pirouettes

How many errors can you find?

# PIROUETTE BALANCING Series

**Purpose:** To challenge your ability to move from one foot to the other and find center.

## Technique Reminders

1. In relevé retiré, your body alignment is centered along its axis directly over its balancing point.

2. Toes are held long and relaxed not clenched or clawed.

3. All elevés/relevés rise to a full demi-pointe.

4. Hold hips and shoulders squarely over the supporting leg.

5. When you relevé to retiré, push off the floor with the lifting foot.

6. Hold feet and ankles strongly in full demi-pointe without wobbling.

7. Hold your knee solidly over your toes when in plié.

### Relevé Retiré with Alignment Square:

Hold alignment square from back of your workbook squarely in front of you. Plié in 5th and relevé pushing off the floor and quickly snatch your leg to retiré. Keep your back stretched and centered with the supporting leg pulled up strongly and the lifted leg well turned out. Check the squareness of your hips and shoulders with the alignment square. Balance 5 counts and return with control. Repeat on the other leg.

### Walking Degagés:

Elevé on R, brushing L through the floor to degagé devant. Posé forward controlling your balance. As you lower your L, begin to degagé R forward.

### Centering Exercise in 2nd:

1    2, 3    4, 5    6, 7    8

Demi plié in 5th, press front foot off the floor lifting knee and hold. Stretch both legs straight 2 counts. Close slowly to 5th plié, straighten, and repeat.

# BASIC TURNING Series

**Purpose:** To test how well you can find center when moving from two legs to one.

**Promenade in Retiré**: From 5th, posé devant into retiré and lower the heel of your supporting foot. Slightly lift that heel off the floor and turn 1/8th en de hour and close to 5th. Repeat until you have completed one full turn. Repeat on the other foot.

**Posé à la seconde (below)**: Demi-plié in 5th and degagé to 2nd. Posé to retiré on the demi-pointe strongly pushing through the floor. Hold 3 counts and return with control to 5th. Repeat on other side.

Be sure your body remains centered

**1/8th Turn Pirouettes**: Start in a narrow 4th with arms in pirouette preparation. Demi-plié and relevé turning only 1/8th. Be sure to push off from both feet and maintain center. Hold 3 counts and spring down. Repeat on other side. When mastered, progress to 1/4, 1/2, and finally singles.

## Common Problems: Why They Happen

1. Leaning forward: Trying to use momentum to rise instead of using the strength in the muscles of your feet, ankles and lower leg.

2. Clawing: Extrinsic muscles working too hard.

3. Reduced height of demi-pointe and/or supporting knee bending: Front of ankle or big toe too tight or calf, ankle and feet not strong enough.

4. Rolling out on little toe: Weak ankle or stiff big toe.

5. Body tilting to the side: Compensation for a lifted hip on the other side.

6. Arches roll when landing in 5th (especially the back foot): Weak foot and ankle muscles.

7. Pain in back of the ankle: Not using intrinsic muscles of the foot so achilles must work too hard.

# Perfecting Your ARABESQUES

## When thinking of ballet, a vision of arabesque comes to mind. It is ballet's signature movement.

### THE PERFECT BEGINNING À TERE

Beginning in 5th with knees stretched. When you tendu derrière, make it more than simply pointing your toe, actively engage your core and turnout muscles. Lengthen both legs and articulate your tendure, shifting your weight to 60/40. Extend your lifting leg outward and upward, lengthening away from your body.

### EXTENSION (the height your lifting leg reaches)

As you begin to lift your working leg, maintain center and continue extending directly behind the shoulder of the raising leg. Lift your core in and up to support, not sink into, your back and avoid pulling your shoulder back as it will pinch in your waist. Shoulders remain square with your hips throughout your arabesque. When lifting your leg past 45 degrees, your pelvis may begin to tilt forward slightly. Avoid lifting your hip up. The amount of arch you achieve in your back varies widely with each dancer. Through stretching and strengthening exercises, you can increase your back's ability to arch making extension higher with balance, and elevé easier to attain.

### LINE

Arms are the final touch in your arabesque. Stretch them long with effortless strength and softened wrists. Feel your arms extending out from below your shoulder blades just as your leg extends from your core. Though some will disagree, in arabesque derrière, I prefer shoulders to remain square in dancers working below an advanced level as it maintains alignment and doesn't encourage the hip to lift and upper body to tilt. Balance the height of your arms with the height of your lifted leg. For together, they create the line your are forming. Add a lovely lifted or inclined head for the final touch to the beautiful picture you are creating.

# Cecchetti and Vaganova ARABESQUES

## Each form of ballet has its own specified arabesques.

### Cecchetti's 5 Arabesques

First Arabesque   Second Arabesque   Third Arabesque   Fourth Arabesque   Fifth Arabesque

### Vaganova's 4 Arabesques

First Arabesque   Second Arabesque   Third Arabesque   Fourth Arabesque

**Enrico Cecchetti (1850 -1928)** was born in a theatre in Rome to dancing parents. He became a famous dancer and one of the greatest teachers in history, teaching the greats of his time like Pavlova, Nijinsky, and Balanchine to mention a few. The Cecchetti graded method of ballet training is internationally recognized. A Cecchetti-trained student has purity of line and simplicity of style with natural turnout, fast footwork, clean lines, and smooth transitions with an emphasis on body line.

**Agrippina Vaganova (1879 -1951)** was a distinguished Russian ballet dancer, choreographer, and teacher. By request from the Russian government, she created her own method of ballet, which is named after her. Her book "Basic Principles of Classical Ballet" (1934) is still regarded as the standard for Vaganova instruction. She was Artistic Director of the Kirov Ballet from 1931 to 1937. Her method encourages great flexibility and extension with high effortless leaps and powerful turns.

# ASSESSMENTS #29 - #36

## #29 and #30 - Relevé Retiré in Parallel
## #31 and #32 - Relevé Retiré in Turnout

| | |
|---|---|
| **Purpose:** | To demonstrate correct placement and balancing skills in relevé retiré in parallel/turnout and hold 3 counts. |
| **Errors:** | Lifting hip and tilting body. Not being able to balance for 3 counts. |
| **Correction:** | Review and practice alignment and balancing exercises. |

## #33 - Posé Développé Devant

| | |
|---|---|
| **Purpose:** | To demonstrate the ability to spring forward onto a strong straight leg and balance for 3 counts. |
| **Errors:** | Lifting hip and tilting body. Not being able to balance for 3 counts. |
| **Correction:** | Review and practice foot/ankle strengthening, alignment, and balancing exercises. |

## #34 - Posé Retiré à la seconde

| | |
|---|---|
| **Purpose:** | To demonstrate the ability to spring into posé on a strong, straight leg with a well placed arabesque, balance for 3 counts. |
| **Errors:** | Stepping, not springing up to posé. Not centered. Unable to hold 3 counts. |
| **Correction:** | Review and practice foot and ankle strengthening, alignment, and balancing exercises. |

## #35 and #36 - Arabesque Combination

| | |
|---|---|
| **Purpose:** | To demonstrate your fluidity, balance, control, and placement when moving from two feet to one, changing directions and turning. |
| **Errors:** | Unable to show the above requirements. |
| **Correction:** | Strength, control, and balance issues. Review material in this book. |

**NOTE: Work Effectively in Each Class You Take**

Incorporate all you have learned from this material in your ballet classes and continue building on this foundation — don't fall back into old habits.

# ASSESSMENTS #29 - #36

| ASSESSMENTS | REQUIREMENTS TO PASS |
|---|---|
| **#29 and #30 - Relevé Retiré in Parallel** | From 6th center floor, plié and spring quickly up to retiré, hold 3 counts without wobbling, losing your center, or demi-pointe height. Spring down to 6th in a well-controlled plié. |
| **#31 and #32 - Relevé Retiré in Turnout** | From 5th center floor, plié and spring quickly up to retiré. Hold 3 counts without wobbling, losing your center, or demi-pointe height. Spring down to 5th into a well-controlled plié. |
| **#33 - Posé Développé Devant R and L** | From 5th (right devant), plié with a degagé devant and posé, springing onto your right leg into arabesque. Hold 3 counts. As you roll down, develop your leg leg devant and repeat on left. |
| **#34 - Posé Retiré à la seconde R and L** | From 5th (right devant) demi-plié with a degagé right to 2nd. Spring into posé bring left to retiré. Hold 3 counts. Spring down left front in a clean 5th. Repeat on left leg. |
| **#35 and #36 - Arabesque Combo Part A** | PREPARATION: Facing 1 in 5th, arms en bas. Tendu right to 2nd bringing, arms en haut. Fouette to face 7 taking arms into 1st arabesque. Raise leg to 90°. Hold balancing 3 counts. |
| **#35 and #36 - Arabesque Combo Part B** | Relevé in 1st ARABESQUE: Demi-plié, relevé holding 3 counts on full demi-pointe, centered with arabesque held at 90°. Roll down maintaining raised leg at 90°. Lower to point tendu, and turn to face front, taking arms to second. |
| **#35 and #36 - Arabesque Combo Part C** | PIROUETTE: Close to 4th back in preparation for single pirouette. End pirouette up and hold. Spring gently into 5th plié and stretch.<br><br>Note: Vaganova points of the room are used. |

# BALANCE DISORDER

## What is a Balance Disorder?

A condition which makes you feel dizzy, floaty, or makes the room spin or tilt, even though you are not moving - this is a balance disorder. This condition may be caused from over a dozen issues which affect the information our brain receives:

- Some health issues such as Meniere's Disease (recurring bouts of dizziness), Mumps and measles (two viruses which can travel to the inner ear and destroy hair cells and nerve endings), inflammation of the inner ear from an infection, tumors or, the most common, age.
- Medications.
- A problem with the inner ear or the brain.

Balance is mainly controlled by the inner ear. Each inner ear contains a structure which is made up of three loops called the semicircular canals. They inform our brain of any movement our body makes or experiences.

## More About the Semicircular Canals

The inside our semicircular canals are filled with jell and tiny hairs. These hairs are connected to nerves. When we change position, the jell moves which in turn moves the hairs activating our nerves and signaling our brain that we are moving. In order to control balance, our brain interprets and processes information it receives from our eyes, joints and muscles and combines it with this information from our inner ear.

# BALANCING PROBLEMS HAPPEN FROM A WIDE VARIETY OF REASONS

Problems with balance can happen from many issues. From our bones or joints to vision, hearing (as previously described) or the central nervous system. Even heart and blood vessels must work correctly for you to have normal balance. Some problems are listed below.

## Vertigo

Experiencing a sense of the room moving or spinning. Vertigo can be caused by many conditions including a particle within the body which comes loose and becomes stuck within the inner ear, migraine headaches, motion sickness, injuries to the head as well as what was listed in the previous page.

## Presyncope

Feeling faint but remain conscious. This can happen from a sudden loss of blood pressure or heart disease.

## Disequilibrium

Feeling imbalanced or losing your balance easily when moving can be caused from inner ear problems, nerve damage, weak or unstable joints or vision problems.

## Lightheadedness

If you breathe very fast and deep, you can hyperventilate or over-breathe. When we breathe too fast, we breathe out more carbon dioxide than we produce, and the level in our blood falls below normal. This, in turn, raises our blood pH causing alkalosis and you feel lightheaded or dizzy. Some medications may also have this same effect. People who suffer from panic attacks sometimes breathe too fast and must breathe into a paper bag to stop this feeling.

## Chapter 7

# About Pointe

Being placed en pointe is the main goal of most young ballet dancers. This, however, is not an easy task for there are technical levels which must be reached. Pointe requires years of training, tremendous foot / ankle strength and flexibility, fantastic balance, and strong core control. If a dancer is allowed en pointe before developing these skills, she will not only have a considerably harder time en pointe but will be much more vulnerable to injury.

# SUMMARY
## Chapter 7
# ABOUT POINTE

It is so exciting to finally be able to purchase your first pair of pointe shoes, and there is a lot to consider to arrive at the best shoe for you. Though fitting these shoes will probably be done by a trained fitter where you buy your shoes, there are several things you should know.

## SHANK:

In the sole of a pointe shoe is the shank which comes in different levels of firmness. A stiffer shank is for dancers with a flexible arch. Less firmness is for dancers with less flexible arches. You also want to be able to roll up to pointe through the demi-pointe and not pop either up or down.

## VAMP:

The length of the box (the vamp) must cover the top of the toes and lie flat not gapping away from your foot nor allowing your foot to budge.

## WIDTH:

The width of the box should fit snugly across your metatarsals with padding. Too loose will not help support your weight and too tight will squeeze your foot.

## LENGTH:

The length of your shoe is generally one size larger than your street shoes. Without padding, stand in 2nd and grand plié to check if your toes barely touch the end. Then place your foot en pointe and pinch the back 1/4 inches. This will allow you to rollup through demi-pointe.

## BREAKING IN YOUR POINTE SHOES:

After you've sewn the ribbons, gently break in your pointe shoes at the top of the arch to make sure it fits snugly against your instep. Breaking in the ball may be needed for stiffer shanks so you can roll up and down.

# the History Pointe

**THE HISTORY OF THE POINTE SHOE IS ALSO A HISTORY OF POINTE TECHNIQUE**

## The Creation of Pointe Shoes

King Louis XIV

Around 1730, dancers, rather than simply moving from pose to pose, began incorporating jumps and leaps in their performances. Ballerinas began rebelling against the movement restrictions their costumes placed on them.

Marie Ann Cupis de Camagro removed the high heels from her shoes and created a scandal by shortening her skirt so as not to hide her intricate foot work like entrechat quatre and cabrioles, previously only danced by men.

Women slowly became more prominent in ballet and their work included more and more jumps, leaps and turns. Ballerinas appeared like Mlle Lyonnalis who was famous for her gargoulliades, and Fraulein Heinel who amazed Europe with her multiple pirouettes - but still on demi-pointe.

Credit for rising en pointe is usually given to Marie Taglioni, but there were previous dancers who occasionally would rise to the tips of their ballet shoes. But, in 1832 Marie Taglioni danced the full length of La Sylphide rising en pointe often, and it was she who developed the technique thus revolutionizing ballet and transforming what was a trick into a means of artistic expression. "Her grace, lightness, elevation, and style earned her an adoring audience and a brilliant career." Taken from the records Gaynor Minden, Inc.

### Before Pointe

In the sixteenth century, Italian princess Catherine de Medici married Henri II of France, and introduced court ballet to the French. These productions with masks and costumes became lavish extravaganzas from which the vocabulary and steps we use today emerged. After Louis XIV became king, he established the first school of ballet in 1661.

# Why Did **BALLERINAS RISE** en Pointe?

In 1796, Charles Didelot achieved great acclaim for choreography in a ballet for which he invented a "flying machine" so it would appear that his dancers were weightless. The machine would lift dancers up on pointe before leaving the ground. This lightness and etherial quality was loved by the audiences, and more choreographers and ballerinas began looking for ways to use pointe work in their pieces.

*The 1830's were the heart of the Romantic age and ballets were full of "passionate but tragic encounters between mortal, terrestrial man and supernatural female." With ballerinas dancing the part of an ethereal spirit or fairy, rising en pointe was the perfect "not bound to earth" effect.*

Premiering in 1845 in London with great expectation, *"Pas de Quatre"* by Jules Perrot became a historic ballet because it featured four of the greatest ballerinas of this time together at one time on stage. In order of appearance was Lucile Grahn, Carlotta Grisi, Fanny Cerrito, and Marie Taglioni. This order was set by age from youngest to oldest to "quelch further confrontations between them." The fifth of the great Romantic ballerinas of this time, Fanny Ester, was invited to dance at this gala event but declined. This ballet captured the Romantic style as these ballerinas danced with delicacy, elegant fluidity, and demure lightness.

# How Ballet Shoes Became Pointe Shoes

In La Sylphide (the world's oldest surviving ballet and often confused with Les Sylphide coming later) Marie Taglioni danced en pointe in shoes that were no more than slightly altered satin slippers. The sole of her shoes were leather with the sides and toe darned to help them hold their shape. Later, ballerinas would pad their toes, but they had to rely on their foot and ankle strength to keep them en pointe for the soles of their shoes offered no support.

The great difference in pointe shoes didn't take place until the late 1800's when Anna Pavlova started placing leather soles in her ballet slippers to make a stiffer shoe to help support her very high arches. It wasn't long before the sharply-pointed toe of Taglioni's time was replaced by a more sturdy flattened toe box made from layers of fabric. Soles and boxes evolved experimenting with cardboards and paste made from flour, to denser glues and boxes of plastic or rubber. By the late 1920's, the modern pointe shoe was in production. Though changing little, they continue to evolve to meet the dancer's needs.

*Marie Taglioni, (1804 -1884) Italian ballerina who's artistry and pointe work changed the art form of ballet.*

*Anna Pavlova, (1881 -1931) Among the greatest of Russian ballerinas, she wore a soft pointe shoe, but reinforced the sole to help support her very high arch.*

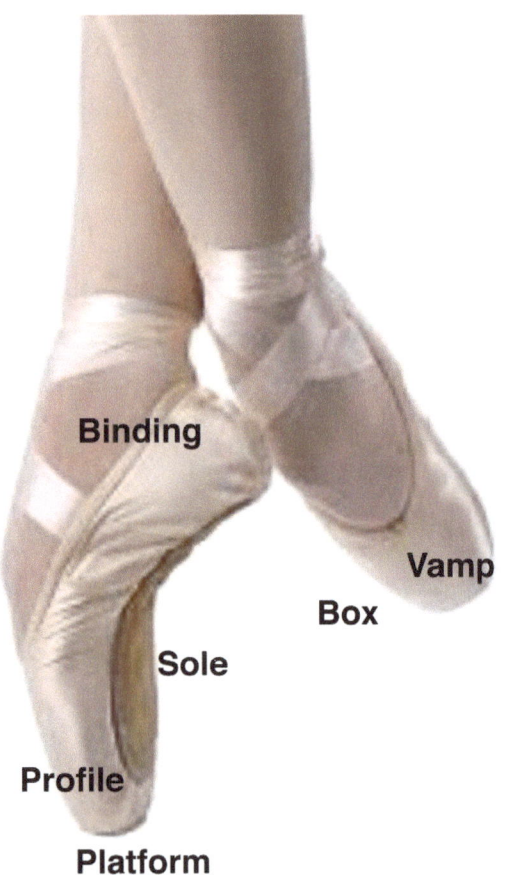

## Pointe Shoe Construction

- The BOX is a stiff cup that encases and supports the toes.
- The VAMP is the height of the box.
- The SOLE is a single piece of leather on the shoe's bottom.
- The SHANK is the insole of the shoe. It comes in various degrees of stiffness to offer foot support.
- The BINDING surrounds and holds the draw string.
- The PLATFORM is the box end.
- The PROFILE is the box width.

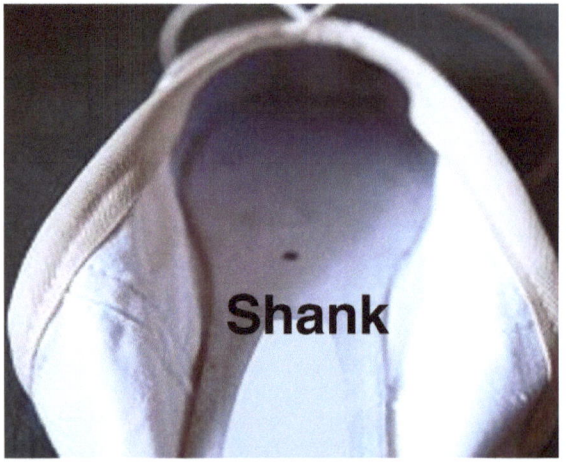

## VARIATIONS IN POINTE SHOES

### BOX VARIATIONS
a. Square – Straighter sides
b. Slight Taper – Sides taper in a little
c. Somewhat Tapered – Sides taper in more.
d. Tapered – The most taper to the platform
e. Winged Box – extra-long stiff sides

### SHANK STRENGTH
a. Medium - Standard firmness
b. Firm - A firmer shank
c. Double Shank - 2x the strength of the medium

### PROFILE VARIATIONS
a. High - Cylindrical in shape
b. Medium High
c. Medium
d. Low - Flat in shape

### VAMP VARIATIONS
a. Long
b. Medium
c. Short

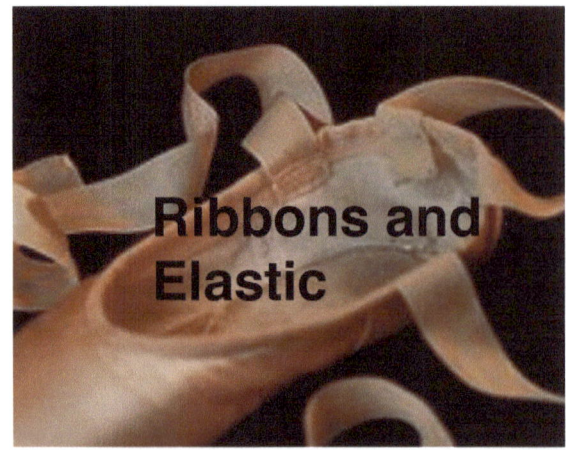

# Fitting Your Pointe Shoes

**Shank:** Beginners usually need a softer shank in order to work through the shoe properly. A softer shank enables the dancer to use her shoes to continue strengthening her feet. Medium density is usually fine. If the shank is too hard, the dancer is either up or down and not able to work through the ball of her foot.

**Box:** 1. The vamp (length of the box) must not be too long or too short as this can be a source of pain. The top and sides of the vamp must extend to the top of the toes and not gap above the foot.

2. Width of the box must be wide enough so the foot slides snugly (with padding) into the box. Toes should be held firmly yet not squeezed together and not so wide as to allow the foot to sink down into the toe.

# Padding for Pointe Shoes

- Should you develop a blister, use medical tape, masking tape or duct tape — whatever you prefer— around toes that become blistered.

- You don't want to use a lot of padding because you want to build callouses on your toes. Too much padding squishes your toes together within the box and is very uncomfortable.

- Types of padding:

    lamb's wool pads
    paper towel
    cut-off pantyhose or socks
    gel toe spacers and tubes for any toe that rubs
    Ouch Pouches: Different sizes
    Gel pads: You can cut them to fit in your pointe shoes, especially on top of
    your toes.

Baby powder helps absorb moisture: With your shoe en pointe, sprinkle baby powder in the toe and tap to spread. Experiment with what works best for you. Try to use the least amount of padding necessary. (Paper towels work well, they are cheap, absorb sweat, and are disposable.) The less padding you use, the better you can balance and feel the floor.

# How to Tie the Ribbons on Your Pointe Shoes

- Put on your point shoes and flex your foot so as to avoid putting too much tension on your tendon.

- Cross the inside ribbon over the front of your ankle and cross the outside ribbon on top.

- Pull ribbons taunt enough so there is no gaping.

- Wrap the ribbons around just above your ankle bone keeping the inside ribbon against your tights.

- Finish with your ribbons meeting on the inside of your ankle between your Achilles and ankle bone.

- Tie a knot and tuck the ribbon ends and knot inside.

# Reasons for Pain and Blisters

1. Feet are too weak.

2. Shoes fit poorly:
    Box is too narrow or too tight (little toe joint bulges from the side of your pointe shoe). Vamp is too long or too short, box too big allowing dancer to sink into the point of shoe.

4. Box rubs on the skin.

5. Toes knuckling (clenching or clawing) inside the box – keep toes long when pointing.

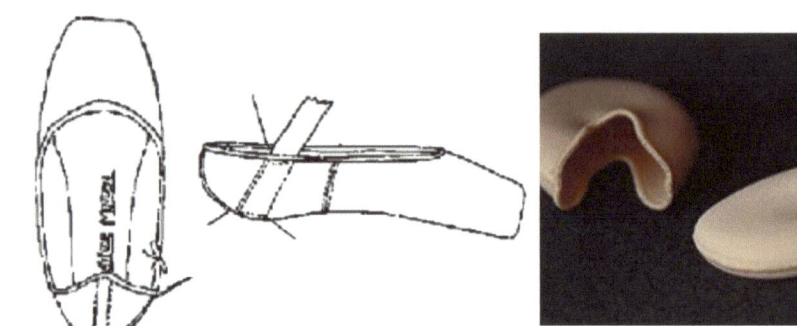 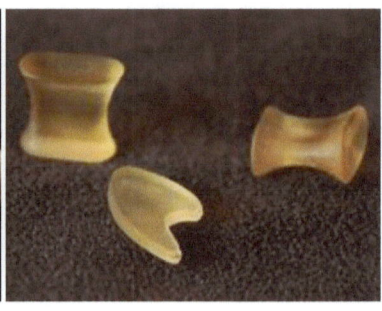

## Attaching Your Ribbons and Elastic:

1. Cut 4 pieces of ribbon, approximately 22 inches each and burn ends to avoid fraying.
2. Find the proper place to attach ribbons by folding down the back of the shoe so it touches the lining. Use a pencil to draw lines at the creases.
3. Place the back edge of the ribbon against the pencil line. The end of the ribbon should be almost down to the lining. Angle the ribbon so that it leans diagonally forward from the heel.
4. With needle and thread, slip stitch the ribbon to binding and lining. Don't sew through to satin.
5. Now the elastic (if your teacher agrees): Wrap elastic comfortably (not too tight) around your ankle include tabs and cut. Place your thumb on the back seam of your pointe shoe. Place one end of the elastic on the right side of your thumb, the other the left side of your thumb and whip stitch in place. Elastic helps the heel from slipping off.

## Breaking in your pointe shoes

Dancers *break* in new pointe shoes to improve the fit and eliminate discomfort.

**Breaking in the arch of your shoe:**
- Turn the heel satin inside out so the inner lining is on top.
- Slide your foot into the shoe with any padding you will use on your toes
- Place your foot en pointe and press down a little (not with your whole weight).
- Grasp the point where your arch ends and your heel begins.
- Remove your foot from the shoe.
- Using the floor, gently press the inside of your shoe's heel downward to the point your fingers have marked. Be careful not to bend your shoe too much. Just soften so the shank fits snuggly along the sole of your foot when en pointe.
- Place your shoe back on your foot.
- The top of the shank should now curve perfectly up under your heel leaving the instep and toe sections straight.
- This curve will help support your heel to stop your foot from sinking down - it will also make the shoe last longer.

**Breaking in the ball of your shoe:**
- With the ball of your shoe on the floor and your thumbs inside on the ball, gently push downward lifting the back up to the demi-pointe line.

# Pointe Shoes and Your Feet

### A HIGH-ARCHED FOOT

Though very attractive, a foot with a high arch can present problems by allowing you to roll over the front of your pointe shoe, which can also cause arch pain. The best shoe is a higher vamp with a 3/4 shank. A hard box will support the foot and prevent it from giving way.

Russian shoes are often better suited for the high arched foot.

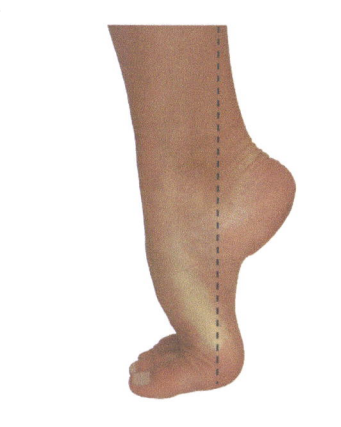

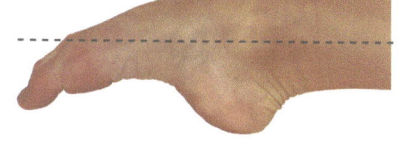

### FITTING INFORMATION FOR ALL FEET

A general rule of thumb in selecting the length of your pointe shoe is to take a length one size larger than your street shoe. Place the shoe on your foot without padding. Try a grand plié in second (this stretches your foot out to its full length) The tops of your toes should barley touch the end of the box and not feel crunched.

Now try the pinch test. Place your foot en pointe and see if you can pinch the back of the heel 1/4" by the draw string. This allows enough room for you to roll up en pointe through the demi-pointe.

The top of the vamp should lie smoothly against your foot and not gap or bulge. It must cover your toes and knuckles through the front and sides. A pointe shoe should hug and not pinch and should be comfortable when standing flat.

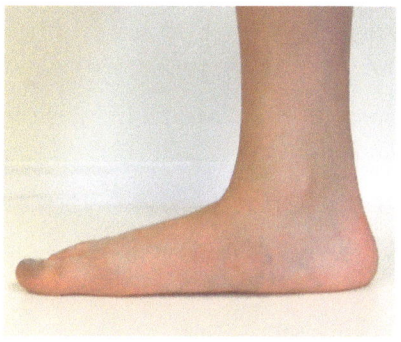

### A LOW-ARCHED FOOT

Low-arched dancers want to find a pointe shoe which maximizes the little arch they do have and hug the bottom of their foot closely. They generally require a supple shank which allows a dancer to rise more easily en pointe. An experienced dancer may choose a 3/4 or split-sole shoe.

### Advice from the doctor:

"Dancers en pointe need strong foot muscles, but more importantly, they need core strength. This helps dancers lift up out of their hips."  Dr. Karen Clippinger

## THE WIDTH OF YOUR SHOES

The width of your feet is measured across your knuckles at the ball of your foot. Your shoe must fit this width properly to help support your weight and not allow you to sink into your shoe. Likewise, you don't want the vamp to be too tight and cramp your feet, either.

## THE DEPTH OF YOUR VAMP

The length of your toes determines the depth of your shoe's vamp. The longer your toes, the deeper your vamp needs to be. This way your knuckles can be fully covered and supported by your shoe.

## ABOUT SWEATING FEET

Sweating feet break down your pointe shoes quicker. You might consider buying 2 sets of shoes and alternating them. Always allow your shoes to dry out before storing. Also, try powdering your feet before putting your pointe shoes on.

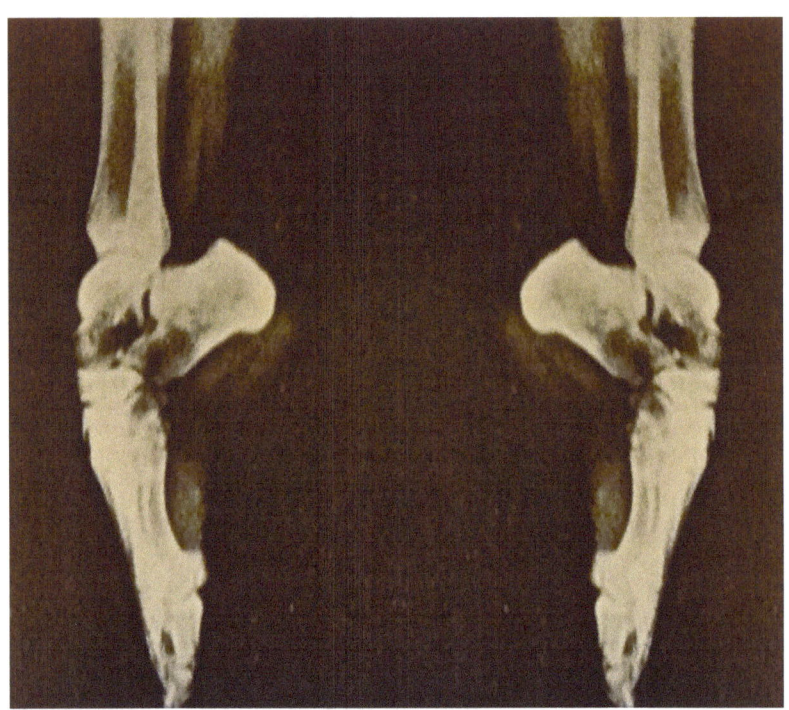

# FLAT FEET AND POINTE SHOES

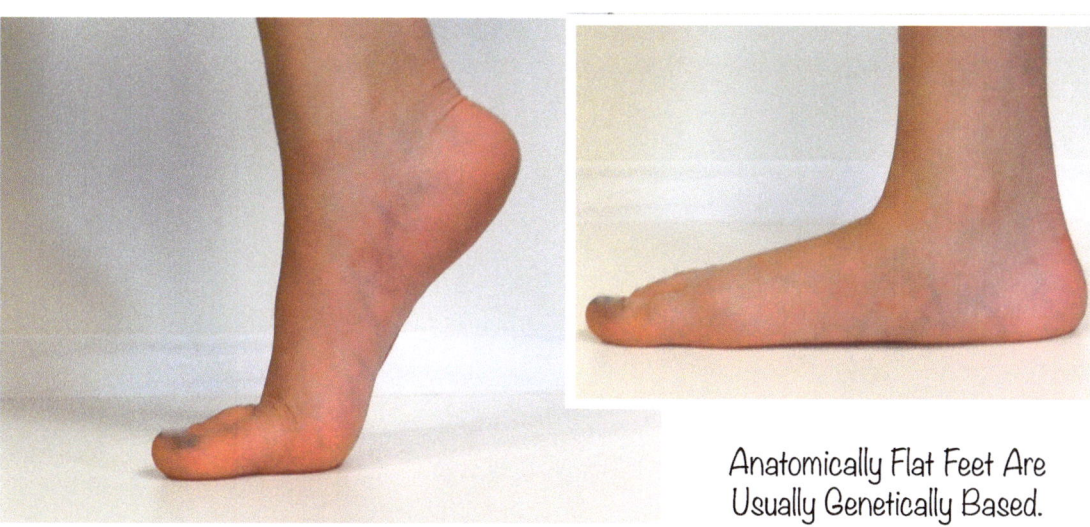

*Anatomically Flat Feet Are Usually Genetically Based.*

## VARIOUS TYPES OF FLAT ARCHES

### THE MOBILE ARCH
This arch has very stretchy ligaments and poor muscular support. It needs a lot of strengthening exercises for the toes and foot to be strong enough for pointe.

### THE FLAT CURVE ARCH
An arch where the shape of the bones establish the arch and no matter how strong the muscles of the foot become the arch won't change very much.

### THE STIFF ARCH
An arch where the ligaments hold the arch rigid with little movement in the foot gives them little shock absorption. A lot of foot stretching exercises are needed before starting pointe.

### THE MOBILE ARCH and POINTE
This type of foot needs a lot of foot and ankle strengthening to become strong enough for pointe. The emphasis needs to be controlling and stabilizing the small muscles beneath the toes and under the foot. Before this is achieved, the dancer must not attempt pointe work.

### THE FLAT CURVED ARCH and POINTE
Pointe work is still possible for a dancer with this type of arch, provided she has good control of the muscles below her foot. This foot won't be as arched en pointe but should be stiff enough for stability en pointe.

### THE STIFF ARCH and POINTE
Because this foot has such little ability to absorb shock, it can be prone to foot and ankle injuries. A great deal of stretching above the top of the foot is necessary before a dancer with this type of foot attempts any pointe work.

# VERY FLEXIBLE FEET AND POINTE SHOES

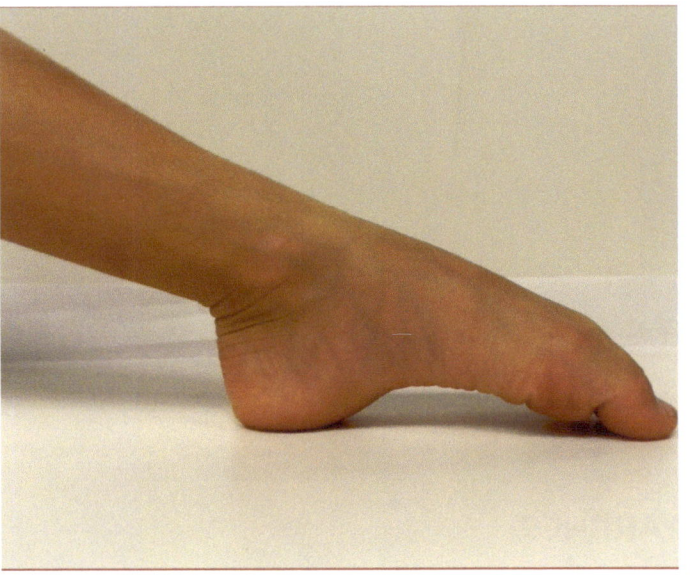 

**Keep working on your foot strengthening exercises from the "Foot and Ankle" section to develop very strong feet.**

- Break your pointe shoes in correctly so the shank fits snugly against the back of your foot and curves outward to hold your heel. If the shank of your pointe shoe is left stiff from tip to heel, your arch will be too far away from the shank. Your shoe will twist away from the heel and not supporting it.

- Vamp Elastic works to extend the vamp of your shoe in a flexible way. This odd elastic sheet can be stretched over the throat of your shoe preventing your foot from popping over the box. It gives you the support of a deeper vamp without compromising your demi-pointe flexibility.

- Try sewing your ribbons a little further forward. This will give further shank support to the sole of your foot.

- You can also tape your foot to reinforce the arch until you develop enough strength in your feet to prevent rolling forward.

# Pain When on Pointe

Pointe shoes can cause discomfort or pain, especially for beginners, but properly fitting pointe shoes greatly reduce these concerns.

**Nail Pain**—Be sure your nails are trimmed straight across and not long enough to bear weight. This being true, nail pain can be caused by ill-fitting shoes.

**Tendonitis**—Pain in front of the ankle is most likely found in dancers with very flexible feet who are stretching the top ligaments. Should you develop this problem, don't try to work through it. You shouldn't have to stop dancing, but you do need to rest the top of your foot. Improve your technique by using your demi-pointe in class and strengthening the muscles within your feet. Be sure the shank of your pointe shoes is strong enough to give support to your foot. As you rise to this new level, ligaments in front of your foot can be stretched.

**Blisters**—Are caused when your skin is rubbed back and forth against the inside of your shoe. Most blisters pop and can bleed in your shoe before you feel much pain. Pain is felt when the raw skin is exposéd. If the flap of skin from your blister is salvageable, apply an antibiotic, replace it to protect the raw area and apply dressing. If not, cut off any dead skin remaining.

Chapter 8

# MISCELLANEOUS INFORMATION AND DAILY IMPROVEMENT SHEETS

# SUMMARY
## *Chapter 8*
# MISCELLANEOUS

Appreciate, respect, and care for your body and the art it is expressing.

## TECHNIQUE:

Technique is the foundation on which dancers build their art. Mastering technique may seem tedious to some, but dance is a performing art, and lack of technique is obvious to observers. The dancer who incorporates excellent technique dances with control, elegance, and confidence as well as safety.

## LINE:

When dancers become aware of the lines their bodies form as they move, they take a giant step forward as a dancer. Line is the difference between so-so and WOW!

## SAFETY:

Even though dancers continue to push themselves to achieve bolder feats, they must hold an awareness of safety. How tired am I? Are my legs shaking? Then proceed with caution for they could give way. How warmed up am I? Do I have the strength/flexibility for this movement? Don't forget about the power of your mind. Accidents can, and do, happen when dancers are distracted.

## HEALTH:

Dancers demand a lot from their bodies. Take good care of them by eating right (avoid junk foods), staying hydrated, massaging out sore areas, and avoiding dangerous substances.

# Technique

A WORD ABOUT

*The Foundation of Dance*

*Very Valuable Basics*

I've had students in class who were simply uninterested in technique - they only wanted to "dance." But DANCE quickly slips away from one's abilities and aesthetics without proper technique. Learning the fundamentals takes a lot of concentration, effort, and determination, even more so after developing bad habits.

Technique, though seeming to limit you, is a tool which sets you FREE. The dancer who is determined to improve her technique will gain the skills, strength, and balance she needs to soar to incredible heights and look gorgeous as well. With a strong technical background, you can achieve greater success in your turns and leaps and are much less likely to experience injury.

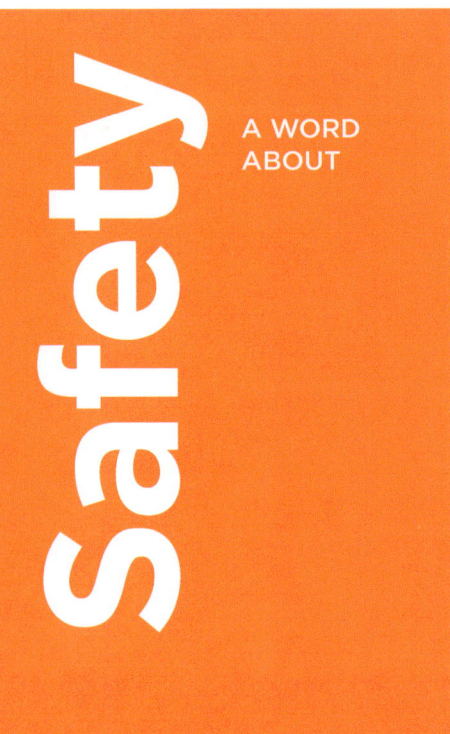

# Safety
### A WORD ABOUT

*This body is the only one you will ever have – treat it well.*

## Take Good Care of Your Body

Remember the four primary reasons for injuries.

- Inadequate strength or flexibility for the movements you're attempting.
- Not properly warmed up for the movements you're attempting.
- Too tired to control the movements you're attempting.
- Lack of concentration and focus on the movements you're attempting.

You will have a much more injury-free dance career by knowing your body and avoiding these pitfalls.

A WORD ABOUT **Health**

Without your health - you have nothing....

## The Benefits of Dance

*"Dancing can be magically transforming. It can make a spirit soar, unleash locked-away creativity; unite generations and cultures; and turn sadness into joy, if only during the dance."*

**AARP**

**DANCE**
- Strengthens bones and muscles
- Tones your entire body
- Improves posture and balance
- Increases stamina and flexibility
- Reduces stress and tension
- Builds confidence
- Stimulates your mind, memory and creativity
- Provides an opportunity to make friends
- Wards off illnesses and depression

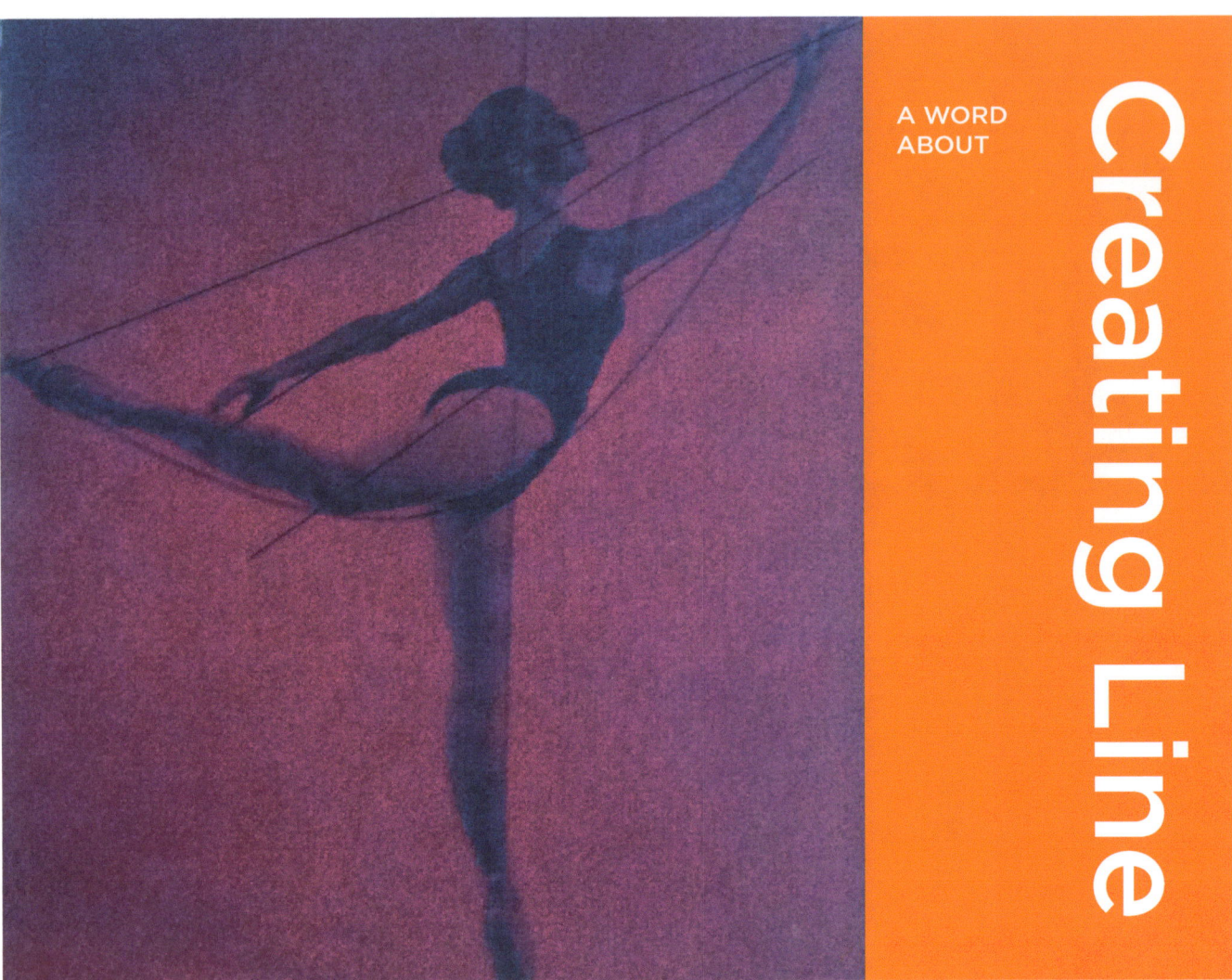

A WORD ABOUT

# Creating Line

## *The Shapes You Form While Dancing*

Become aware of the shapes you create with your body as you dance. The placement and curve of your arms, the carriage of your head, the lift and angle of your leg, the directions you face, all form the visual picture you create as you dance. Every line means the difference between awkwardness or elegance, so-so or sensational. Start looking critically at yourself in the mirror. Discover what adjustments will make you look better and incorporate them in your work.

*The difference is all about line!*

Every dancer is unique not only in bodily proportions, strengths, and flexibility but in the delivery of their movements. Everyone can create a beautiful line simply by remaining aware of their placement.

# MUSCLE SPASMS and CRAMPS

**Muscle Spasms:** Rapid, uncontrolled muscle contractions that occur when a voluntary muscle (one that you control) contracts on its own.

**Cramps:** If the force of the spasms contraction is very strong, however, it's a cramp. Cramps are prolonged and painful.

Cramps can happen from failure to stretch, muscle fatigue, lack of oxygen, extreme heat, dehydration, or not enough salt and/or minerals like magnesium in your system.

Leg cramps are more common in adolescents, adults over 65, and heavier people.

Should a cramp strike you, stretch the cramping muscle opposite to the contraction. For example, should you get a cramp in your calf, quickly flex your foot away from the contraction by pressing your heel downward in a lunge or take hold of the ball of your foot and pull it toward you. It is very important to stay hydrated and eat a well-balanced, healthy diet with the appropriate levels of minerals.

**Sometimes muscles deep inside our body start cramping.** The iliopsoas muscles can cramp up, this feels like an achy low back pain spreading outward, sometimes even into the gluteal and outer hip region. A key indicator that you have a cramping iliopsoas is when you rise from a seated position and find it difficult to stand upright. Extending the leg makes it worse. Doing too many sit ups or working hard on your turnout in développé devant extensions, even sitting too long can cause the iliopsoas to spasm. Trigger point therapy and stretching have been found to be very helpful for spasms.

# DEHYDRATION

Between 60% and 70% of our body is made up of water. It plays an extremely important roll in the maintenance of our body as it transports nutrients, removes waste, and maintains our temperature. Our bodies release water in several ways which the average person needs to replace with around 2.4 liters of water per day. Athletes (including dancers), however, lose a dramatic amount of water from sweat and exhaling moisture from their lungs - much more than the average person.

**The Pinch Test to see if you are dehydrated:** Pull up a small amount skin on the back of your hand. If it falls back quickly, you're fine. If it lingers in a ridge and takes time to fall back, you need more water.

**The Weight Test to measure the amount of water you lose in class:** Step on a scale before and after class. If you've lost 1 pound, you need to replace that loss with one 16 oz. bottle of water.

To avoid dehydration, take a water bottle with you into class and place it below the barre where you are working. Without making a disturbance, take sips during breaks in your class work.

## Symptoms of Dehydration:
- Thirst
- Tiredness and lethargy
- Decreased performance
- Cramping
- Fatigue
- Nausea and vomiting

*NOTE: If you ever experience severe cramping and nausea go immediately for emergency help.*

*NOTE: Don't think that a soft drink containing caffeine is hydrating you. It actually is pulling water out of your body because it's a diuretic.*

**Water and Our Brain:** Nutritionist Glenn Cardwell in his blog "Water for the Brain" recounts studies where children, who were given water 20 minutes before taking cognitive tests, out-performed those who were not given water. This proves that increased hydration helps mental performance. Mr. Cardwell also notes that an adult's ability to think starts to decline when they are 1% dehydrated. For example, a 140-pound adult can lose up to 3 cups water from his body.

# MAKING SMART FOOD CHOICES

Dance is a mind-body art form that requires both physical and mental sharpness. The demands it takes for a dancer to stay healthy and strong and perform at their best level is wisely supported by a balanced, nutritious diet which fuels both the body and mind efficiently. A good diet is essential for building and keeping physical strength, stamina, agility, and the lean muscle dancers need, as well as the mental focus, sharpness, and concentration necessary for a top performance. Young growing bodies need proper nutrition. By learning what to eat, and following that knowledge, you will set the stage for a strong and healthy life.

**CARBOHYDRATES** help maintain blood-sugar levels, supply our bodies with fiber, vitamin B and are our main source of energy. For top performance, carbs should make up about 45-60% of a dancer's diet. Carbohydrates are divided into two categories - simple and complex, based on their chemical structure. Our bodies treat simple carbs (white flour, pasta or soda pop) like sugar, creating a short burst of energy then dropping off. Complex carbs are considerably healthier. They break down much slower than simple carbs so their energy is released more slowly at an even rate with no spike (whole wheat flour or pasta, brown rice, and beans). When you begin a dance class, carbs are the first to be burned. After about 20 minutes of exercise, our bodies start burning stored fats.

**FATS** should make up about 20 - 30% of your diet. As with carbohydrates, there are fats which are good for you and others you should stay away from. Good fats supply your body with energy and are essential to your health, while bad fats increase cholesterol and risk of diseases.

TRANS-FATS - (fats found in milk chocolate and chips) are difficult for our body to break down and can collect in our arteries, which can lead to stroke and heart attack.

MONO-SATURATED FATS - (olive oil, natural nut butters, nuts and avocados) are much healthier and are necessary to boost your immune system.

**PROTEINS** should make up about 10 -15% of your diet. They are the building blocks of our body and the perfect choice for an after-class snack. (low fat meats, fish, nuts, eggs, and dairy products).

**VITAMINS and MINERALS** are important even with a balanced diet. The demands dance places on your body robs it of important nutrients, and supplementing your diet is vital. A good dietary plan consists of taking a high-quality, multi-vitamin daily and additional supplements as needed and advised by your doctor. Iron and calcium deficiencies are not uncommon among dancers, and it is important to be sure you keep these levels high to avoid problems with your health and well-being. We have all known of dancers who have suffered injuries, even fractures. No dancer ever wants to take time off for an injury. But female dancers are in a high-risk group for low bone mineral density, stress fractures, and stress reactions. Nutrition plays a big role in helping you prevent and manage this type of injury.

## EAT SMALLER MORE FREQUENT MEALS

When a dancer goes too long without eating or restricts energy (calorie) intake, the body is forced to find an alternative source of energy to keep it, and the brain, working. In this state (negative energy balance), your body actually lowers your metabolic rate and breaks down your muscles by turning them into the fuel it needs. Starving the body results in less muscle, a lower metabolic rate, and a higher percentage of body fat. Plus the dancer is more fatigued and has less energy with which to dance. Eating smaller, more frequent meals boosts your metabolism, and keeps your blood sugar stabilized.

## CUT DOWN ON SUGAR

We may be born with a sweet tooth, but cultivating it can lead to long-term health problems. Here's some advice for cutting down on sugar.

Choosing to eat sweet snacks over healthy foods can lead to excessive weight gain and can result in more complicated problems, including diabetes, heart disease and arthritis. Too many sweets can also cause tooth decay and unhealthy gums.

"Because of a decade-long obsession with low-fat consumption, we have managed to fill our store shelves with food that's fat-free but loaded with sugar. The result is a steady increase in the amount of sugar eaten inadvertently through processed foods. Americans are the worst: on average, each American eats 19 teaspoons of sugar per day, whether it's incorporated into foods by manufactures or added themselves. As people become accustomed to sugary foods, companies have to make new products even sweeter. It becomes a vicious circle." from an article in ivillage.

## SECRET SUGARS

Are you aware of the hidden sugar found in many products? From tomato sauces to hot dogs, sugar can be found in the ingredients of many, if not most, of the processed foods you eat.

Sugar is a good source of energy, but processed sugars provide no nutrients and should only be a very small part of a balanced diet. Craving sugar can last a lifetime, but you can change. You can develop a preference for the natural taste of unprocessed, unsweetened foods. Fruits naturally contain sugar but it's accompanied by a healthy dose of vitamins, minerals and fibre. Developing a preference for the sweet taste of fruits is a great alternative to sweeties and baked goods.

**Try replacing sugar syrups with alternatives** such as maple syrup, agave nectar, or pureed fruit.

**Don't make desserts a regular part of every meal:** Save them for special occasions or an occasional treat.

**Top your cereals with fresh fruit:** Replace sugar with fresh fruit, which adds a natural and healthy sweetness to a bowl of cereal. Have you ever thought of putting nuts on your cereal? I really like it, and it gives me some morning protein.

**Become an avid food label reader:** Better yet, put the free FOODUCATE app on your cell phone. Scan the bar code before you buy a product and it will tell you how good the product is by giving it a grade. Sugars listed on labels are a combination of naturally occurring sugar and added sugar. If you spot the ending - 'ose' on a word, it's sugar in disguise. Examples are sucrose, glucose and fructose. Other common ingredients that are sugars in hiding include syrups, honey, brown sugar, fruit juice concentrate, and high-fructose corn syrup. My rule of thumb is to not buy any product that has sugar listed as the first two ingredients or containing two or more sugars.

**Don't get yogurt with fruit in it (have you seen the amount of sugar there?):** Try eating it plain or mix in your own fresh fruit with it - greek is great. You can also create smoothies with plain yogurt and fresh fruits.

**Don't drink juices or sodas:** "Shine" (of YouTube) tells us that "Liquid sugar (their name for sodas) is the easiest way to mindlessly ingest 22 teaspoons of sugar a day. Sodas and juices are loaded with sugar and have little to no nutritional value." Diet sodas increase your sugar cravings. Instead swap your sodas and juices for WATER. Add a squeeze of lemon, lime or orange, if you like. A nurse once told me that this will aid your body in assimilating water and it tastes good, too.

**Drink water:** This sounds simple, but many of us don't do it.

**The easiest way to cut down on sugar:** Eat whole grain breads, fruit and vegetables as often as possible.

**Bring your own snacks:** Mindless snacking puts a lot of unwanted sugar and salts in your body. Fill a baggie with veggies to bring it to the studio for a between-class snack instead of chips, cookies or candy.

**Reduce processed carbs:** White breads and pastas are loaded with "bad" carbs. It may not seem like you're eating sweets, but these carbs convert into sugar soon after they enter your body. Also, note that there is no nutritional value in processed carbs. It was recently on the news, as well as on a Dr. Oz show, that our wheat has been genetically altered and now contains a high-glycemic load, which rapidly converts to sugar in our body and is stored as fat on our belly. Worse yet, belly fat is usually visceral fat which produces hormones that cause our body to produce more fat and cause us to crave more sugar.

**Remember, your diet can either be an extremely slow poison, or the best of all medicines.**

# ADDICTION

These human bodies of ours can become addicted to almost anything (though I can't imagine an addiction to vegetables). Some people are more vulnerable than others. I think the important thing we want to remember is the difference between NEED and WANT. I don't mean the kind of NEED where you need a new pair of jeans. I mean the kind of NEED where your body is screaming for something and won't let you rest until you have it.

If you WANT something, it's just something you would like to have. If you NEED something - you have to have it. When the latter becomes the case, closely consider addiction and see if you can do without it. If doing without makes you really uncomfortable, then you probably have an addiction.

Beside the major problems - drugs, alcohol, and cigarettes, there are a lot of other things that can grab hold of us. Some dancers develop an eating disorder by mistakenly believing that eating very little will make them thin. Instead this addiction makes them weak and unhealthy. Healthy eating is mandatory, especially when taking many classes each week.

Sugar is addictive. OH, NO! Alas, it's true. The more your taste buds have sugar, the more they want it. And boy, does our society push sugar. Not only for the holidays, with cakes and candies, but we find hidden sugars in cereals, snacks, power bars, etc, etc, etc, - in most packaged foods - just read the labels. Try your hardest to limit sugar for only special occasions.

The sad thing about addiction is that it's like feeding a hungry animal inside of you that never gets full. You may be able to put it to sleep, but it's always going to be there. If you feed it, again, it will wake up and want more.

In Pointe Magazine, Zachary Whiterburg (June/July 2012 issue) wrote about a 19-year-old dancer realizing she was addicted to cocaine and it was ruining her life. "We saw professional dancers doing it, and we wanted to be cool like they were." "Cocaine has a long history in ballet," writes Mr. Whiterburg noting Gelsey Kirkland's book, *"Dancing on My Grave."*

The important thing is not to get suckered into trying addictive substances in the first place. Those who pressure you into trying them are not your friends. Remember, it isn't **COOL** - it's **SAD**. AGAIN - take care of your body, and it will take care of you.

# What Are Trigger Points?

Normal healthy muscles don't have trigger points, also known as muscle knots. Trigger points are irritated spots in a muscle that are associated with lumps you can feel in tight bands or nodules within the muscle's fibers. They are tender to the touch (they can even can cause a local twitch) and have a predicted pain pattern. Should you develop one of these hyper-contracted bands/nodules, they can be broken down through pressure from fingers, elbow, tennis or golf balls, rollers or many other self-help tools. Whatever tool you use, stop and hold the pressure on these tender areas in order to deactivate them. Pressure must be held until the pain leaves and the tissue releases. Then you can go deeper or look for other points in the cluster. Once a trigger point has been deactivated, you can roll the muscle to bring some blood flow back to the area, and then stretch the muscle out completely.

Why care about trigger points? Well, they hurt and can cause weakness in the muscle that has them. This changes the way you move. And changing the way you move places a greater load on other muscles, which in turn can develop trigger points.

**NOTE: Not all tender areas are trigger points. Points may be tender if a tissue has decreased blood supply or has been scarred.**

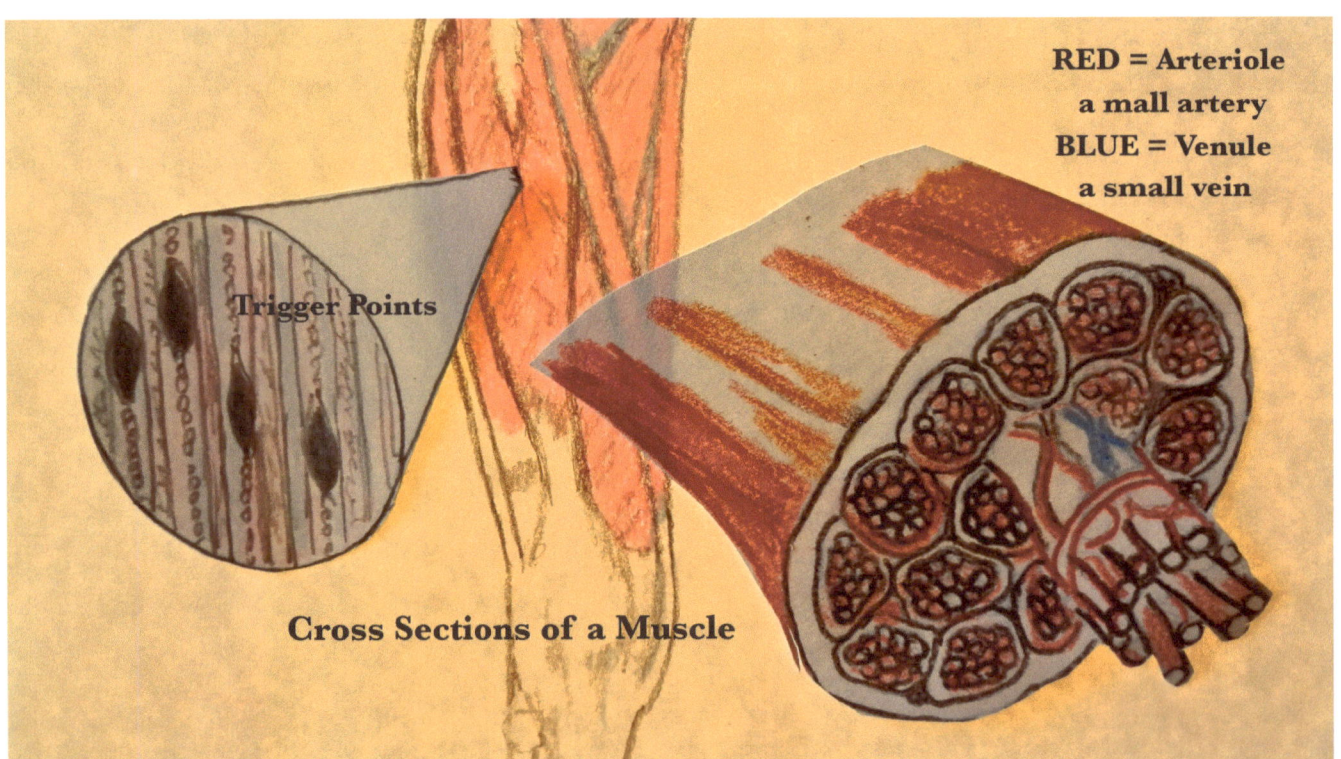

*Unexplained points of pain frequently radiate from trigger points to surrounding or even distant areas. Practitioners claim to have identified reliable pain patterns which link pain in one location to trigger points in another location.*

These tight bands of muscle, which produce pain, are caused from injury, repetitive use, tension, or stress in that muscle. There are other ways of dealing with trigger points besides using pressure, manipulation, and stretching. Some chiropractors recommend a "Spray and Stretch" technique where the muscle is sprayed with a vapocoolant which counteracts the pain while the muscle is stretched to inactivate the trigger points. Anther method is ultrasound with massage and/or injections. AAFP states, "Trigger-point injection has been shown to be one of the most effective treatment modalities to inactivate trigger points and provide prompt relief of symptoms."

These supersensitive bundles can create headaches if located in the neck/shoulder area, intense low back pain if located in the hip or lower back muscles, and decreased range of motion when affecting muscles of the arms or legs.

It is important to understand why these trigger points have developed, if they formed from overuse, tension or stress, and try to elevate the cause. Examine your technique to see where an imbalance exists. For example, in développé devant and à la secondee, are you overusing your quads? Try consciously using and strengthening alternative muscles to ease the load on the one that developed trigger points. Stretch out these trigger point areas on a daily basis. Perhaps work on releasing stored tension and stress in your life.

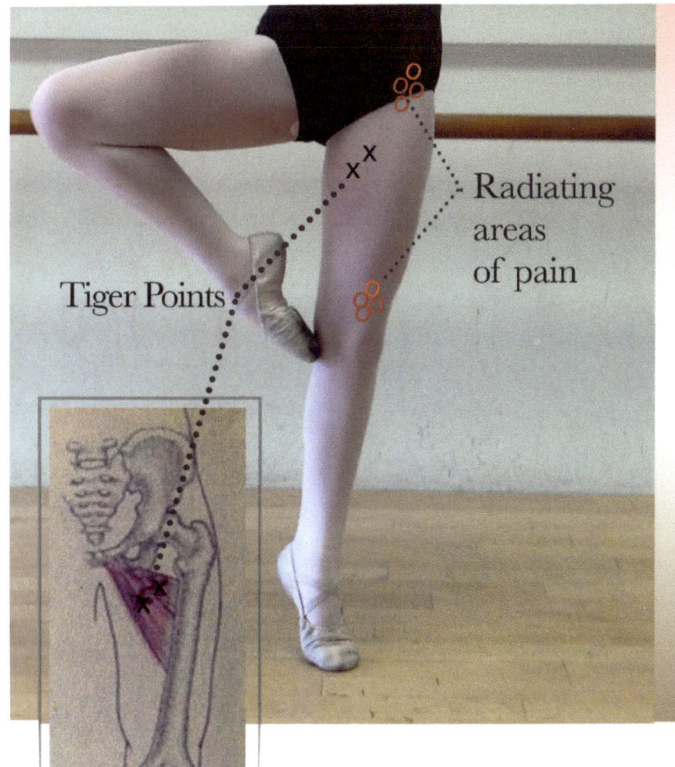

## Trigger Points in the Adductors

A very important part of movement and stabilization in the hips and legs is with the Adductors. Care against injury and over use is equally as important here as with the care of the quads and hamstrings.

Trigger points in the Adductors Longus and Brevis can create pain deep in the groin which can radiate downward to the knee.
They can cause weakness and decreased flexibility in these areas.

# POSTURE AWARENESS

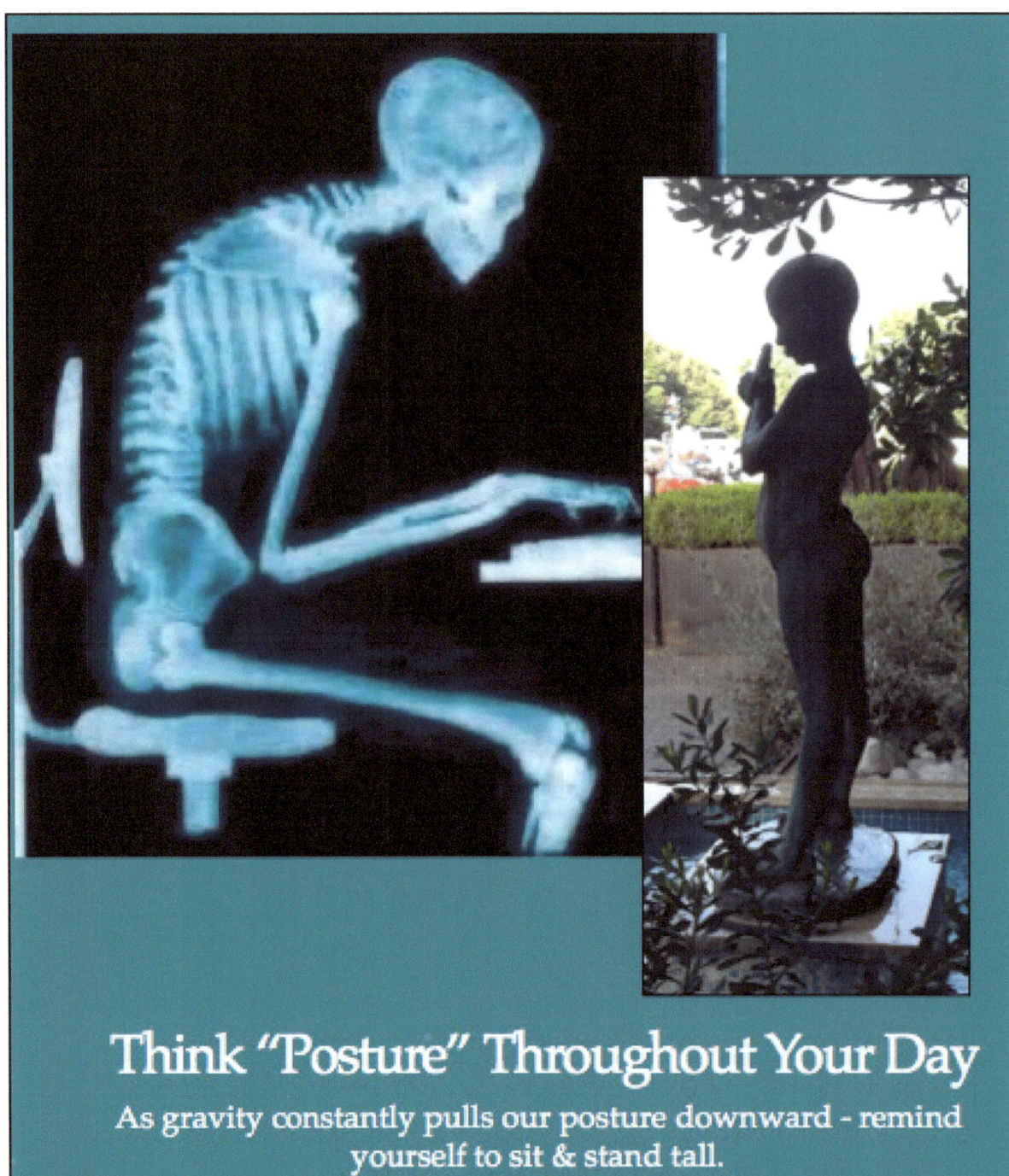

# BALLET DEFINITIONS for Pre-Pointe Dancers

**Demi** - half

**Plié** - to bend

**Tendu** - to stretch

**Retiré** - a withdrawn movement

**Degagé** - disengaged

**Développé** - to unfold

**Echappé** - to escape

**Sauté** - to jump

**Port de bras** - carriage of the arms

**Changement** - to change

**Balancé** - balancing

**Jeté** - a throwing step

**Temps levé** - a raised movement

**Pas de chat** - step of the cat

**Adage** - a slow controlled movement

**Grand** - large

**Petite** - small

**Battement** - beating

**en Croix** - in a pattern of a cross

**Rond de jambe** - circling of the leg

**Frappé** - to strike

**Relevé** - to rise

**Passé** - to pass

**Sur le cou-de-pied** - at the ankle

**Devant** - in front

**Derrière** - in back

**Dessous** - under

**Dessus** - over

**Changé** - with a change

**Allegro** - quick fast movements

# COUNTING IN FRENCH

**Un** - one  **Deux** - two  **Trois** - three  **Quatre** - four  **Cinq** - five
**Six** - six  **Sept** - seven  **Huit** - eight  **Neuf** - nine  **Dix** - ten

# BODY MOVEMENT Terms

**Flexion**

To bend at a joint and decrease the angle between two bones.

**Extension**

The opposite of flexion. Opening the angle between two bones.

**Abduction**

Moving away from center or the midline as in raising your arms to 2nd or spreading your fingers apart.

**Adduction**

Moving back toward center or the midline, as in lowering the arms.

**Protraction**

Moving a body part forward like jutting your chin forward.

**Retraction**

Moving a body part backward and in pulling your chin back to neutral.

**Circumduction**

Moving a body part in a circle as in making circles with your arm.

**Medial rotation**

Rotating a body part on its axis so the front surface turns toward center.

**Lateral rotation**

Rotating a body part on its axis so the front surface turns away from center.

**Pronation**

Rolling inward as in rolled ankles, also rotating the forearm so the palm faces back.

**Supination**

Rotating the forearm laterally so the palm faces front.

**Inversion**

Moving the foot so the sole faces upward.

# MUSCLES and Their Functions

**extensor digitorum brevis**

Allows the big toe to flex upward and reinforces the action of the extensor digitorum longus located in the front of the shin.

**fibularis (pereoneus) longus**

Attached to the fibula bone and located on the outside of the lower leg enabling the foot to point and flair. It also supports the arch of the instep.

**anterior tibialis**

A thick muscle, which enables the foot to flex and is used with every step. It also flairs the foot. It becomes tender if you have shin splints.

**posterior tibialis**

Also in lower front of the leg. It helps point and sickle the foot.

**vastus medialis—VMO**

A large inner-thigh muscle which is a part of the quads. It mainly extends and stabilizes the knee.

**rectus femoris**

The powerful quad muscle which extends the knee and flexes the thigh to the pelvis.

**sartorius**

A long narrow, flat muscle which lifts and turns out the thigh. It also helps bend the knee.

**adductor longus**

A long muscle enabling the thigh to turnout, draw into center, and flex at the hip.

**tensor of fascia lata—TFL**

A thick muscle in front of the hip. It keeps the knee extended and lifts the leg. A tight TFL can limit turnout.

**rectus abdominis**

A flat muscle known as the "six pack" which flexes the trunk forward as in doing sit-ups.

**external and internal obliques**

Large thin muscles enabling the trunk to flex and rotate.

**transversus abdominis**

The deepest of the abdominals, it stabilizes the torso. It is mainly made of slow-twitch fibers.

**extensor digitorum longus**

A long muscle located in the lower leg allowing the small (not the big toe) toes to extend. It also helps the foot to flex.

**flexor digitorum longus**

A long muscle located in the lower leg which pulls the small toes downward.

**flexor hallicus longus**

A long muscle located in the lower leg which pulls the big toe downward.

**flexor hallicus brevis**

A small two-headed muscle located under the foot which flexes the big toe.

**soleus**

A large flat muscle located beneath the gastrocnemius, which extends down the back of the lower leg merging into the Achilles tendon enabling the foot to point and the heel to lift up. It is a major muscle used in walking, running, and jumping.

**gastrocnemius**

A two-headed muscle which forms the curve of the calf and allows the foot to point and flair.

**piriformis**

A muscle located deep inside the back of the pelvis along with other smaller muscles. It is important for turnout from the hip.

**iliopsoas**

Located deep in the pelvis comprised of the psoas major and minor, and the iliacus.

**gluteus maximus**

The largest outer muscle in back of the pelvis, it is used to extend the hip as in walking up stairs or running.

**gluteus medius and minimus**

Smaller muscles located on the upper side of the hip one on top of the other. They are important in stabilizing the hip.

**adductors**

A group of muscles located on the inside of the thigh which draw the leg inward, lift, and help with turnout.

**quadriceps**

A four-headed muscle located in the front of the thigh. It extends the knee.

**hamstrings**

Three muscles located in back of the thigh that flex the knee and extend the thigh, as in grand battements, derrière, attitude, and pas de chat.

**trapezius**

A large flat triangular-shaped muscle of the back which allows shoulder and head movements.

**latissimus dorsi**

A large flat triangular-shaped muscle located below the trapezius that controls movement of the shoulder and shoulder blade. It also extends, pulls back, and rotates the arm.

# Acknowledgments

Inspiration for creating this book came from my desire to have a complete source of materials, beyond regular ballet classes, which would give dancers the knowledge and understanding needed to build their skills for a sound foundation en pointe.

What a fantastic age we live in! Much of the material covered on the science behind movement was not available to dancers so many years ago. Yet, even now, tried and true techniques from the past have proved viable and have changed little. My goal, through much research combined with my own 50 years of teaching experience and knowledge gleaned from my teachers, was to create an interesting and understandable document which young dancers could not only use to strengthen, correct, and improve their technique and understanding of their bodies in preparation for pointe, but as a reference for future use, as well.

I owe a great deal to the work of Lisa Howell, physiotherapist, dancer, teacher and creator/director of "Perfect Form Physical Therapy" of Sydney, Australia. Her writings have enlightened dancers, teachers, and parents in the science behind movement and her criteria for pointe inspired and set the foundation for the development of this book.

Two other people I must acknowledge. My husband, Charles Reeder, for his total support and encouragement, and Sandra Ishida, director and founder of Pacific Coast Academy of Dance, for creating the atmosphere from which this pre-pointe program could evolve.

*Inadequately prepared dancers who are placed en pointe not only face a discouraging, frustrating experience but are dangerously exposéd to the possibility of injury.*

# Bibliography

1. Lisa Howell. Dancer, teacher, physiotherapist, writer and founder/director of "Perfect Form Physiotherapy" in Sydney, Australia. Newsletters and "Perfect Point" book.

2. Phases of Movement. Wikipedia, the free encyclopedia. Chris Goulet, Google article 1/12/04. Chris Duffin on Concentric training Animal-Kingtom-Workouts.com.

**Youtube**

3. Butterfly Picture .................................................................It's an amazing WORLD out there
4. Hip Pain..................................................................................................... Your Hip Pain
5. Dancer........................................................................................ Ballet Dancer Pictures
6. Hyperextended Knee ...................... Yoga Journal - Yoga Anatomy - The Hyperextended Knee
7. Hypoextended Knees Picture ........................................................... PhysioAdvisor Anatomy
8. Calf Anatomical picture................................................................... Expert Running Guide
9. Muscles of the body .............................................................................. Human Muscles
10. Stretches for the top of the foot ............................................Stretches for the top of the foot
11. Plantar Fasciitis.............................................. Orthoinfo Healing Solutions for Plantar Fasciitis
12. Trigger Point Illustrations ............................................... anatomyfacts.com/muscle/tpill,htm#
13. Injuries and Foot and Ankle Pain ...........................................................................WebMD
14. Clicking Hips .............. Rudolf Nureyev Foundation Medical website Lisa Howell's Newsletter
15. Trigger Points Adductors ........................ Rhino Fitness Latest Article "Got Pain? Don't Wait!
16. Calf Strengthening Series ..................................................................... RunnerDude'sBlog
17. Pointing your foot................................ Patrick Wenning, MPT, CIMT How to Point Your Foot
18. About the Shoulder Blade........................................... Winged Scapula/LIVINGSTRONG.COM
19. Anatomy.Pictures ...................................................................................................WebMD
20. Balance and Pirouettes...............................................................................Physics of Dance
21. Parts of a Pointe Shoe................................................................................ A Dancer's Word
22. Low Back Stabilization............................... NISMAT - Low Back Pain Stabilization Exercise

23. Core Stability ................................................................ Science Direct "The myth of core stability"

24. Extension Ballerina ................................................................................. Ballet Pictures

25. Mid Back Muscles .............................................................................. Holistic Well-being

26. Pointe Requirements ..................................................................... All About Pointe Article

27. Ingrown Toenails ..................... PubMed Health Mayo Clinic St. Bernardine Medical Center

28. Plantar Fasciitis ........................................................................ Lisa Howell, Dr. Oz, Web MD

29. Turned Ankles ..................................................................................... Alan S. Woodle, DPM

30. Flat Feet ....... Can I go on pointe if I have flat feet? - Lisa Howell Flat Feet - PubMed Health

31. Bunion Picture ................................................................................................... WebMed

32. Pictures of rolled and neutral ankles .............................................................. My Flat Feet

33. Muscles and What They Do ................................ Merrian-Webster Visual Dictionary Online

34. Fast-Twitch/Slow-Twitch ...... How Do Fast-Twitch and Slow-Twitch Muscle Fibers Influence

35. The History of Pointe ................. History of Pointe Shoes and Technique by Gaynor Minden

36. Scoliosis.. ....................... Rehabilitation School for Scoliosis, Scoliosis Rehabilitation Center

37. Balance Disorders ........ National Institute on Deafness and other Communication Disorders

38. Flat Feet ................. AllExpertsBallet /Pointe Dancers with Flat Feet Ballet Blog, Lisa Howell

39. Cramps and Spasms .................................................................... Dynamic Chiropractic

40. Posture Awareness .......................................................................... Spine Anatomy Models

41. Nutrition ...................................................................................................... Livingstrong.com

42. Pain in the back .................................................... Livingstrong.com, Common Back Injuries

43. Nutrition ........................................................................................................................ ivillage

44. Trigger Points: Diagnosis and Management ..................... American Family Physician /AAFP

45. Balancing Problems ................................................................................................ Mayo Clinic

# OUR DANCERS

I am so very grateful to all our dancers who very graciously gave of their time and talents in posing for pictures within this book. It has been such a pleasure working with all of you.
**Miss Carol**

**Dancers listed in alphabetical order:**

- Makena Angus
- Gabrielle Blackwell
- Sammi Chapin
- Faith De Neve
- Chloe East
- Caroline Greene
- Krysta Hansell
- Riley Hersch
- Andie Lane
- Caroline Lobber
- Taegan Mehrens
- Hannah Olsen
- Gigi Russell
- Ella Schoenig
- Devyn Shanley
- Hanna Stolrow
- Reese Valeriano
- Hanna Talieh
- Lindsay Backer
- Kendal Carney
- Sadie Cook
- Taylor Chen
- Samantha Dwyer
- Hailey Flowers
- Margaret Greene
- Nadia Hawkes
- Savannah Isaacs
- Ashley Lobber
- Ava McCoy
- Lany Newman
- Jessica Ringer
- Kennedy Santini
- Delaney Shanley
- Danielle Silver
- Paris Smith
- Alexa Rae Vano

*Photography by Carol Reeder and Jason Green*

# ABOUT THE AUTHOR
*Carol Reeder*

I was a knock-kneed, five-year-old with rolling ankles. So my mother enrolled me in ballet to remedy this situation, and I've been a part of the dance world ever since.

Throughout my grammar and junior high school years, I studied with Mona Francis, a Cecchetti teacher, in Whittier, California, where I took my Cecchetti student exams. In high school, I studied in Los Angeles with Rosalie Frey, a student of Anna Pavlova, and a very "hands-on" teacher —a trait I use to this day. In high school, I organized, choreographed and wrote skits which were top place winners in the school's Hi Jinx All- Girl Skit Competitions. At U.C.L.A., I majored in dance.

After college, I moved to Whittier where I taught ballet and tap at a local studio, danced professionally in *The King and I*, and completed my Cecchetti teachers exams to the Licentiate level. Five years later, I opened my own studio (The Carol Odom School of Dance) in Hacienda Heights and later a second one in Whittier.

I've been with Pacific Coast Academy of Dance under the direction of Sandra Ishida since its inception where I'm an Academy instructor and head up their pre-pointe program.

*Teaching Through Time*

Hint - I'm in the back row.  FIRST PLACE

"Pot Luck," Carol Abrahams, director

*Miss Carol then and now*